Safeguarding
in the
Classroom

Safeguarding
in the
Classroom

Debbie Innes-Turnill

1 Oliver's Yard
55 City Road
London EC1Y 1SP

2455 Teller Road
Thousand Oaks
California 91320

Unit No 323-333, Third Floor, F-Block
International Trade Tower
Nehru Place, New Delhi 110 019

8 Marina View Suite 43-053
Asia Square Tower 1
Singapore 018960

Editor: James Clark
Assistant editor: Esosa Otabor
Production editor: Martin Fox
Copyeditor: Ritika Sharma
Proofreader: Girish Sharma
Indexer: TNQ Tech Pvt. Ltd.
Marketing manager: Lorna Patkai
Cover design: Sheila Tong
Typeset by: TNQ Tech Pvt. Ltd.
Printed in the UK

© Debbie Innes-Turnill 2025

Apart from any fair dealing for the purposes of research, private study, or criticism or review, as permitted under the Copyright, Designs and Patents Act, 1988, this publication may not be reproduced, stored or transmitted in any form, or by any means, without the prior permission in writing of the publisher, or in the case of reprographic reproduction, in accordance with the terms of licences issued by the Copyright Licensing Agency. Enquiries concerning reproduction outside those terms should be sent to the publisher.

British Library Cataloguing in Publication data

A catalogue record for this book is available from the British Library

ISBN 978-1-5296-8020-1
ISBN 978-1-5296-8019-5 (pbk)

To Evie – my inspiration

Contents

About the Author ix

Acknowledgements xi

Introduction xiii

1 **Your Role as Part of the Safeguarding Team** 1

2 **Knowledge and Understanding of Safeguarding** 15

3 **Building Relationships as a Foundation for Safeguarding** 33

4 **Safeguarding Communication** 49

5 **Well-Being** 65

6 **Behaviour as Communication** 79

7 **Emotionally Sensitive Strategies** 93

8 **Creating a Safe Environment** 111

9 **Early Help – What Does This Mean for You?** 123

10 **Teaching Safeguarding to Children and Young People** 139

11 **Online Safety** 153

Conclusion 163

Index 165

About the Author

Debbie Innes-Turnill has been a Teacher/School Leader for over 30 years. Her second degree, in Psychology, followed by an MSc in Advanced Child Protection Studies has enabled her to develop an expertise in the support and protection of the vulnerable and their families. In her last school role she was the designated safeguarding lead – developing the whole school culture of safeguarding and ensuring that children, young people and the school were kept safe. She now lectures part time at the University of Birmingham in Child Protection and has begun a PhD in Safeguarding Culture in Education. Her other academic research interests are related to children living in poverty, children's experiences of trauma and how their needs are met. She also has a keen interest in safeguarding and equality, diversity and inclusion.

In addition, in 2018 Debbie launched her own freelance safeguarding consultancy, which complemented by her school experiences, advises schools, charities and other organisations in safeguarding culture. She provides a holistic approach to the well-being of both children and adults thinking about their participation to improve practice in keeping them safe. This work is underpinned by her own research and that of her colleagues.

Acknowledgements

I would like to thank all the people who have made this book possible. Firstly, thanks go to Rachel Eperjesi and Colin Forster – you encouraged me to write and introduced me to Sage.

Thank you to Lisa Lea-Weston, Evie Innes-Lewis, Andy Sprosen and particularly Toby McGregor who read chapters and gave me a sense that I was on the right track and encouraged me onwards.

A particular thanks goes to all the children and young people that I have worked with, who have inspired me and taught me so much about how they need to be supported in order to learn.

The team at Sage who believed in me from the start and provided guidance and support.

My family who have always believed me and gave me the space to write.

Introduction

This book is the handbook for safeguarding for teachers. Safeguarding is often spoken of as 'everyone's responsibility'. As a busy class teacher this can be difficult to manage. This book provides a practical guide to manage all aspects of safeguarding in a busy teaching role in order to keep all children and young people safe.

Safeguarding can be a difficult and traumatic aspect of a teacher's life. There may be ideas, concepts and experiences in this book that are difficult or perhaps even distressing. If you are triggered by anything that you read, it is important that you put the book down and seek support from your professional colleagues or others. We cover how you look after your own well-being and build supportive networks to support your emotions in Chapter Three.

The book includes case studies developed from the experience of the author in all phases and types of schools. They capture the essence of real cases without being identifiable unless they are taken from published information, in which case that information is referenced. The case studies and in places other information are followed by reflective questions that you are encouraged to think about to aid understanding and improve your practice.

Throughout the book safeguarding issues, abuse and neglect, trauma and welfare needs are referred to. These are used interchangeably unless there is a specific reference being used. This is because schools use these terms loosely to cover the entirety of safeguarding. Exact definitions for safeguarding, child abuse and neglect are provided in Chapter Two. Trauma is defined in Chapter Seven.

In places the language of victim and perpetrator are used. Where this refers to adult perpetrators and child or young person victims, it indicates the power differential in the relationship. This becomes more difficult when the abuse is 'child-on-child' and has been avoided where possible and so should you.

A Brief History of Safeguarding in Education

It is important to situate the safeguarding that teachers have to manage in the context of how we arrived at this point. Schools have always had the welfare of their pupils at heart. Over time, the concern for welfare has become more formalised. The failure of schools to share information along with the lack of social work understanding of schools was criticised including in the review of the death of Maria Colwell in 1974. This case led to a number of changes in legislation and guidance throughout the 1970s and

1980s aimed at ensuring all those working with children worked together (Baginsky et al., 2022). This culminated in *The Children Act* (UK Government, 1989) along with the companion *Working Together Under the Children Act 1989: A Guide to the Arrangements for Inter-Agency Co-Operation for the Protection of Children From Abuse* (Home Office et al., 1991) which for the first time formalised the role of a number of agencies' involvement in child protection. This included schools.

Further acts of parliament: *The Children Act* (UK Government, 2004) and *The Children and Families Act* (UK Government, 2014) combined with further statutory guidance in the guise of *Working Together to Safeguard Children* (Department for Education (DfE) 2006, 2018, 2023) have contributed to the guidance that all those working with children have to follow in order to prevent the abuse of children. Somewhere in the midst of this development child protection became safeguarding which broadened the definition of the responsibilities of agencies including schools.

In 2014, statutory guidance was introduced specifically for schools. *Keeping Children Safe in Education* has been updated yearly since its introduction. Its comprehensive and now extensive coverage intends to enable all schools to provide a consistent standard of safeguarding. This plethora of instruction enables schools to fulfil their obligations with respect to safeguarding and provides a check system to ensure that they are compliant.

How This Book Helps You to Fulfil Your Safeguarding Duties

The book is set out in the following chapters to support your important role in Safeguarding in the Classroom.

Chapter One – Your Role as Part of the Safeguarding Team

This chapter sets out the role of a class teacher in the bigger school picture. It introduces the other roles and how communication should happen in order to ensure that children are kept safe. This practical information enables knowing who to speak to and when.

A simple flow diagram summarises the process for ease of reference.

Chapter Two – Knowledge and Understanding of Safeguarding

This chapter explores the knowledge you need about safeguarding as an essential part of your classroom safeguarding culture. While it does not replace the need for you to read *Keeping Children Safe in Education* or the school safeguarding policy it helps you pick your way through this technical document and retain the information that is essential for daily work with children and young people. The Prevent strategy is introduced with a critical analysis of the problems that teachers encounter with it.

Chapter Three – Building Relationships as a Foundation for Safeguarding

Relationships between children or young people and staff, between staff and between staff and the children or young people's parents are the foundation of safeguarding culture. This chapter sets out why and how relationships, trust, professional love and communication ensure that abuse and trauma is found out and prevented. It supports you in developing the positive relationships with children and young people that are needed for them to be safe and secure and therefore share their experiences and feelings.

Chapter Four – Safeguarding Communication

This chapter looks at the specifics of how to communicate with others about safeguarding. It includes how to record concerns, how to speak to children and young people and how and when to speak to their parents. You will be able to develop your ability to have difficult conversations that have a lasting impact on the lives of the children and young people in your care. It also covers how to maintain a professional relationship through communication with children, young people and their families, particularly in relation to social media use.

Chapter Five – Well-Being

Staff and pupil well-being are intrinsically linked. This chapter explores the link and sets out what needs to be in place to safeguard well-being across the school – including examples of how schools can address well-being. It also looks at how you can recognise when you need support and where to go to get that support. How some teachers are supported through supervision is also introduced. This chapter also makes clear the difference between well-being and safeguarding so that you are clear when and how to refer.

Chapter Six – Behaviour as Communication

Everything we do says something about what we are thinking and feeling. This chapter sets out how an understanding of this leads to a safeguarding approach rather than a traditional behaviour management approach. Understanding what children or young people are saying through their behaviour is set out as a means for discovering abuse over and above traditional disclosure.

Chapter Seven – Emotionally Sensitive Strategies

Trauma-informed and shame-sensitive practices are introduced alongside attachment awareness and the concept of Adverse Childhood Experiences (ACEs). These strategies are now being implemented in classrooms in order to support children who have experienced abuse or damaging experiences. Linking closely to Chapter Six, this chapter explores how to manage the behaviour of children and young people who have experienced challenges in their lives.

Chapter Eight – Creating a Safe Environment

We can all think of places that make us feel safe and cherished. The challenge is how to do this in a classroom environment. This chapter explores options for creating a safe classroom where all children and young people can flourish and those with safeguarding needs, trauma or abuse are able to learn. There is also a focus on Equality, Diversity and Inclusion although this is a thread that runs through the whole book.

Chapter Nine – Early Help – What Does This Mean for You?

Spotting issues before they result in harm is key to safeguarding culture. This chapter sets out what you can look for and your role in an effective early help/early intervention structure. It includes how to build effective partnerships with parents and others to support children, young people and their families. An effective system is explored including how to use an early help assessment tool.

Chapter Ten – Teaching Safeguarding to Children and Young People

A key element of safeguarding which is often under explored is what children need to know and how they are taught about it. This is explored here including how to encourage children to take responsibility for their own safeguarding and that of their peers. The idea of pupil leadership is encouraged with strategies for how this can be introduced.

Chapter Eleven – Online Safety

This chapter looks at the very real problems that teachers encounter not only in the classroom but beyond it in terms of online safety. It explores the issues around keeping children and young people safe on school networks and the issues children and young people encounter with each other both in school and out of school that impact on relationships with peers. It also covers your role in providing and reinforcing messages about how to keep safe online and how you can do this for yourself to protect your personal and professional identity.

References

Baginsky, M., Driscoll, J., Purcell, C. and Manthorpe, J., Hickman, B. (2022) *Protecting and Safeguarding Children in Schools*. Bristol: Policy Press.

Department for Education (DfE) (2006) *Working Together to Safeguard Children*. London: DfE. Available at: https://www.familieslink.co.uk/download/june07/working%20together%202006.pdf [Accessed 1.6.24]

Department for Education (DfE) (2024) *Keeping Children Safe in Education*. London: DfE. Available at: https://www.gov.uk/government/publications/keeping-children-safe-in-education–2 [Accessed 26.5.24].

Department for Education (DfE) (2023) *Working Together to Safeguard Children*. London: DfE. Available at: https://www.gov.uk/government/publications/working-together-to-safeguard-children–2 [Accessed 26.3.24].

Home Office, Department of Health, Department of Education and Science and Welsh Office (1991) *Working Together Under the Children Act 1989: A Guide to the Arrangements for Inter-Agency Co-operation for the Protection of Children from Abuse*. London: HMSO.

UK Government (1989) *Children Act 1989, c. 41*. London: HMSO. Available at: www.legislation.gov.uk/ukpga/1989/41/contents [Accessed 26.3.24].

UK Government (2004) *Children Act 2004, c. 31*. London: HMSO. Available at: www.legislation.gov.uk/ukpga/2004/31/contents [Accessed 26.3.24].

UK Government (2014) *Children and Families Act 2014, c6*. London: HMSO. Available at: https://www.legislation.gov.uk/ukpga/2014/6/contents/enacted [Accessed 26.3.24].

1

Your Role as Part of the Safeguarding Team

> **Chapter Aims**
>
> - To set out what your responsibilities for safeguarding are.
> - To explore other roles in the safeguarding team.
> - To think about how you ensure children are kept safe.

Introduction

This chapter sets out the role of a class teacher in the bigger school picture. It introduces the other roles and how communication should happen in order to ensure that children are kept safe. This practical information will enable knowing who to speak to and when. It sets out a holistic approach which goes beyond compliance.

A simple diagram will summarise the process for ease of reference.

Context

In *Keeping Children Safe in Education* (Department for Education (DfE), 2024) and *Working Together to Safeguard Children* (DfE, 2023), the two statutory pieces of guidance that we will look at in more detail in Chapter Two, it is made very clear that 'safeguarding is everyone's responsibility'. The following diagram summarises how this is enacted in the vast majority of schools and where the role of the class teacher fits in all of this (Figure 1.1).

We will begin by exploring what this actually means for you as a class teacher before looking at the other roles in school. Whichever type of school you work in and whatever phase you teach, there are some fundamental responsibilities which you need to know about in order to keep children safe in your classroom.

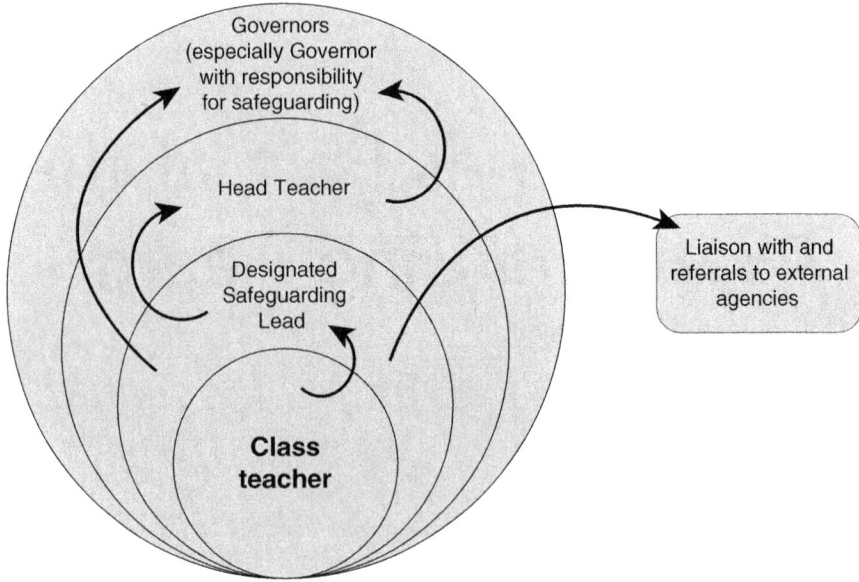

Figure 1.1 The safeguarding system in schools

The Class Teacher

First of all, let us think about you as a class teacher. Whether you are in a primary, secondary, special or independent school you will have the closest relationships with the children or young people in the classes that you teach. Being a good classroom safeguarding practitioner means building good relationships, listening to children's communication whether it be verbally or through their behaviour and making sure you follow the systems in place in your school to keep those children safe. Chapter Three explores how to build relationships. Chapter Four explores how to listen to children and Chapter Six explores behaviour as communication. There are also contractual obligations that you need to know about – particularly those in the *Teachers' Standards* (DfE, 2011 – see box) and also in your school's 'Code of Conduct' document – you will need to make sure that you are familiar with this.

> ### Teachers' Standards: Part Two: Personal and Professional Conduct
>
> Teachers uphold public trust in the profession and maintain high standards of ethics and behaviour, within and outside school, by:
> - treating pupils with dignity, building relationships rooted in mutual respect, and at all times observing proper boundaries appropriate to a teacher's professional position;

- having regard for the need to safeguard pupils' well-being, in accordance with statutory provisions;
- showing tolerance of and respect for the rights of others;
- not undermining fundamental British values, including democracy, the rule of law, individual liberty and mutual respect and tolerance of those with different faiths and beliefs;
- ensuring that personal beliefs are not expressed in ways which exploit pupils' vulnerability or might lead them to break the law.

Teachers must have proper and professional regard for the ethos, policies and practices of the school in which they teach, and maintain high standards in their own attendance and punctuality.

Teachers must have an understanding of, and always act within, the statutory frameworks which set out their professional duties and responsibilities.

(DfE, 2011 p14)

Reflective Questions

Read through these professional standards – which ones do you think are relevant to safeguarding?

We will come back to them at the end of the book to see how you view safeguarding now and whether this has changed your view of these personal and professional conduct requirements.

On a more practical level you need to make sure that you have the knowledge you need to recognise when a child or young person has been abused; this is covered in Chapter Two. You then need to make sure that if a child or young person has disclosed abuse to you, or you are at all concerned for the well-being or safeguarding of a child or young person that you *immediately* follow the process laid out in the school's safeguarding policy. The immediacy of following the safeguarding policy is often difficult in the classroom but delaying can increase the risk for the child or young person. We talk about how you can ensure that support is obtained as quickly as possible in Chapter Three.

The safeguarding or child protection policy, along with the code of conduct and part one of *Keeping Children Safe in Education* (DfE, 2024) are the other documents that you *must* read. Many schools have long and detailed policies which can take a while to read – make sure that you take time to do this, so that you know who and how to report to when needed. All of this should also be covered in the safeguarding training that you must undertake, both when you start at the school and on a regular basis during your tenure. Schools provide this in very different formats so you may have to ask what they want of you, particularly if you join mid-year. A checklist is provided at the end of this chapter detailing what you need to know to take up your role as part of the school's safeguarding team.

Once you have referred on any disclosures you may not be involved in the detail of what happens next. However you will, most likely, continue to teach the child or young person so it is important that you continue to build the relationship you have with them.

If you have concerns that do not meet the child protection threshold (see Chapter Two) you may need to carry out actions in order to support the child or young person. The responsibility of the class teacher for this varies from school to school which is why you need to read the safeguarding policy, so that you know exactly what the expectations are. *Keeping Children Safe in Education* (DfE, 2024) states that class teachers are in part responsible for Early Help and we will explore this in Chapter Nine but some of the examples below would fall into following up concerns rather than Early Help.

Case Study 1.1 – Class Teacher Responsibility Examples

Example 1 – Mary has nits, you have noticed this before and asked her Mum to make sure that she treats them. You know it is your responsibility to speak to Mum again and make sure that she knows how to treat the nits.

Example 2 – Joseph looks very sleepy in your lesson – he falls asleep towards the end of the session. You know it is your responsibility to speak to his Dad and let him know that Joseph has fallen asleep in class and ask if there is anything that school needs to know about.

Example 3 – You become aware that Janine is not eating any lunch – she is in your class and you think she is supposed to be bringing a packed lunch to school. When you try and talk to her about it she gets very upset and says she forgot to bring it today. You know it is your responsibility to ring her parents and ask them what they know about the packed lunch.

Example 4 – Malaki does not have the correct equipment with him for your lesson, this is the third time in as many weeks. When you ask him about it he says he just forgot. You know it is your responsibility to ring his carer and ask if they can remind him to bring the equipment to school.

Reflective Questions
- Would you feel confident to have these conversations with parents or carers?
- Who could you ask if you needed support to have these conversations?
- What might the outcome of these conversations be? Have you thought about scenarios and what you would do depending on what is said?
- Do you know what you should do if, when you have these conversations, something is disclosed that means that the child is at risk of harm?
- What safeguarding issues can you identify?
- How might you apply this case study/learning with the children and young people that you work with?

If you do have concerns that meet the child protection threshold or a child makes a disclosure of abuse, then you need to refer this on to the Designated Safeguarding Lead (DSL). How you take a disclosure and what you write in the referral is covered in Chapter Four.

Overall you are responsible for the behaviour, emotions and safeguarding of the children and young people in your class or classes and these needs have to be addressed before children can learn. While you do not have to shoulder this responsibility alone you will be the person who is closest to the children or young people in your care, so make sure that you know how to take on this responsibility. This book can act as the foundation for your understanding which will need to be part of continuing professional development throughout your teaching career.

Next, we will look at the role of the DSL and other members of the safeguarding team in your school.

The Designated Safeguarding Lead and the Safeguarding Team

Every school has to have a Designated Safeguarding Lead often referred to as the DSL – their role is laid out in Annex C of *Keeping Children Safe in Education* (DfE, 2024). They are responsible and accountable for leading and managing safeguarding culture in the school and should be a member of the Senior Leadership Team (SLT). This means that they determine the strategy and policy (which is approved by governors). They are responsible for making sure that all staff have the safeguarding knowledge they need. They are responsible for making sure that any child or young person with safeguarding needs is supported and referrals are made to external agencies in a timely fashion – hence the need for you to refer onto them *immediately* when there has been a disclosure or you have a safeguarding concern. Their accountability means that should something go wrong for a child or within the school with regards to safeguarding they are held responsible. They should also be contactable throughout the school day – ensuring that all staff know how to get hold of them if they are needed. Depending on the level of safeguarding need in your school there may also be an out of hours or school holiday contact. Again this should be laid out in the safeguarding policy so make sure you know who and how to contact, storing any numbers you may need in your phone.

The DSL is also responsible for: ensuring that record keeping conforms to the regulations, filtering and monitoring standards are adhered to (we will cover your responsibilities in respect of this in Chapter Eleven), supporting staff and establishing relationships with external agencies. In order to do all this, they will have received enhanced training to help them carry out their role.

Case Study 1.2

Sarah started working at a small secondary school halfway through the year as an Early Career Teacher (ECT). She was provided with copies of the staff code of conduct and the safeguarding policy before she started and made sure that she read these. She completed the online safeguarding training that she had been sent the link for and took the subsequent certificate into school on her first day. She also met the DSL who was also one of the Assistant Head Teachers on her first morning in school.

The reality of safeguarding in the classroom was quite different from what Sarah had seen in the training. She felt quite unsure as to whether issues were things that she should deal with or whether they should be referred on to the DSL.

The DSL had made it clear that she could talk to him whenever she needed to make sure that she got the balance right. When a young person in one of her Year 10 classes told her that he was not happy at home and that his older brother had been arrested the night before Sarah went to the DSL and asked what she should do. The DSL told Sarah that he already knew about the child's older brother but that Sarah should upload what the child had said to her so that his voice was captured on the system. The DSL helped Sarah to think about what she was going to write and how to continue to support the child with his feelings in class. The DSL also alerted the child's other teachers so they could watch out for any adverse effects from his experience.

Reflective Questions
- Think about how well you know the DSL and how confident you would feel about approaching them when you are unsure what to do.
- How can you make sure that a safeguarding issue is not missed because you are not sure what to do?
- What safeguarding issues can you identify?
- How might you apply this case study/learning with the children and young people that you work with?

While every school will have a DSL whether there are other individuals who take responsibility for safeguarding is up to each individual school and there are many and varied ways in which schools organise themselves. The most common way is for schools to have one, or more, Deputy Designated Safeguarding leads – known as DDSLs. These individuals support the DSL by managing referrals, information systems and so on but do not hold the organisational accountability that the DSL holds – they will however be trained to the same enhanced level as the DSL. Larger schools will have Safeguarding or Pastoral Teams made up of the DSL and DDSLs along with, perhaps: Attendance Leads, Family Support Workers, Behaviour Support, Mental Health leads and Special Educational Need Coordinators (SENCOs). It is important that you find out who is who in your school and how the safeguarding system works. That way you will know who to speak to when you need to rather than finding out when you have a disclosure to discuss. Meeting the DSL and any others involved in the management of safeguarding should form part of your induction as you saw in the case study. If it does not – make sure you ask to meet them, preferably after you have read all the documents you need to read (see the checklist is provided at the end of this chapter). It might be useful to ask the questions in the box to ensure you are secure about what you need to do.

> ### Questions to Ask the Designated Safeguarding Lead
>
> - Is there anything you think I should know about my responsibilities for safeguarding in this school? (Make it clear that you are compliant in having read the documents in the checklist at the end of this chapter. Make sure you ask for the standard safeguarding training if you have not received it).
> - What are the most common safeguarding needs in this school?
> - Can you help me understand what you want me to follow up and what needs to be referred to you?
> - Can you clarify any other responsibilities I will have with regards to Early Help?
> - Is there any extra support for me as a new teacher in this school when managing safeguarding in the classroom?
>
> ### Reflective Questions
> - Think about how the DSL answered your questions and what this means for your safeguarding practice in the classroom. What else do you need to know to feel confident in managing safeguarding issues in this school?

The Head Teacher (or Principal)

In some schools, the DSL and the Head Teacher are one and the same. This is becoming less common as the DSL role has become enhanced and children and young people have increasing needs. However, in many small schools there are not enough people to have a separate DSL so the Head takes that role too. Even in large schools the Head Teacher is often 'qualified' as a DSL or holds the role of DDSL in order to ensure that they understand all the safeguarding issues in their school and so that they can act to support the DSL. This is particularly important when there is a child protection issue for a child or young person which the school thinks another agency needs to act on and has not. The Head Teacher is able to advocate for the child or young person and DSL as a 'more senior' person in the organisation. In addition to this 'escalation' role the Head Teacher is also responsible for leading the vision and culture of the school – safeguarding culture has become an important aspect of this in recent years. While schools determine this for themselves the Head Teacher will be key in this and supporting the DSL to lead it. The Head Teacher will also be responsible, along with the Governors, for the school's budget and how it is spent, including what is allocated to supporting children or young people with safeguarding needs. Reporting to the Governors about safeguarding in the school will also often fall to the Head Teacher.

Importantly the Head Teacher is also responsible for managing any child protection issues related to members of staff in the school. These are referred to as 'allegations' and are covered in more detail in Chapter Two. As the most senior member of staff, any allegation is referred to the Head Teacher *not* the DSL. They may also be the person who is named to receive 'low-level concerns' (again, more detail in Chapter Two) – make sure you have also read this policy if it is separate from the safeguarding policy.

Whether you meet the Head Teacher regularly will depend on the size of the school you work in. You should be introduced to them as part of your induction. If you are not, then ask the person who has been assigned as your mentor or contact if you can meet them. Better to do this early on than to have to meet them in the first instance during an allegation or low-level concern.

We have detailed here the role of the Head Teacher, or Principal as they are often referred to in Multi Academy Trusts (MATs). In these MATs there is often another level of leadership perhaps including a Chief Executive Officer (CEO) and in some a Safeguarding Lead. If you are working in a MAT make sure you know who these people are and what their role is in safeguarding.

Case Study 1.3

Joseph was walking to break duty when he witnessed one of the teaching assistants restraining a child from Year 8. The child was shouting and yelling while the teaching assistant had wrapped his arms around the child's chest from behind, holding the child into his body. When the teaching assistant saw Joseph he let the child go. The child immediately ran away and the teaching assistant laughed and said to Joseph 'nothing to see here'.

While Joseph was on break duty he thought about what he had seen and decided it made him feel uncomfortable. Although he had not received restraint training he did not like the way that the teaching assistant was holding the child tightly across the chest.

At the end of the school day he went to see the Head Teacher and explained what he had seen. The Head Teacher asked Joseph to write down what he had seen so that she could investigate further and thanked him for coming to see her so promptly. She told Joseph that she would ring the Local Authority Designated Officer (LADO) who would help her navigate through the investigation and any subsequent actions. She told Joseph that it would be unlikely that he would know anything further about the issue but if he had any concerns or worries regarding the incident then he could arrange to talk to her at any time. She told him that it was important that he maintained professional confidentiality about the issue and that he should not talk to anyone else in school about what he had seen or the referral. If anyone else were to ask he was to refer that information on to her.

Reflective Questions
- What did Joseph see that made him concerned?
- Do you feel confident that you would know what to do if you saw one of your colleagues do something that made you feel uncomfortable?

- What safeguarding issues can you identify?
- How might you apply this case study/learning with the children and young people that you work with?

The Governors

The last group of people that you need to know about who are firmly embedded in the school and its culture of safeguarding are the governors. This group of people is responsible for setting the overall vision and strategy for the school. They too have to have safeguarding training and one of them will have training similar to that of a DSL. This person takes responsibility as the safeguarding governor in order to maintain a strategic oversight of safeguarding in the school while all the governors are accountable for safeguarding within the school.

In today's education landscape with MATs there are often a range of governance structures starting with trustees – who to all intents and purposes carry out the same function as governors do in more traditionally managed schools. Many schools then have some form of local governance where the safeguarding oversight of the individual school sits.

While you are unlikely to meet the governors or even the governor with responsibility for safeguarding, it is always useful to know who the people are who set the direction for the school.

The responsibilities for these senior leaders in school and in the local authority are now set out in *Working Together to Safeguard Children* (DfE, 2023).

Case Study 1.4

In Louise's school she has not yet had the opportunity to meet the governors. However, she has made sure that she knows the name of the chair of governors and the safeguarding governor. She has asked the DSL if she can meet both of them if they come into school so that she is familiar with them should she ever need to contact them. She knows how she would contact both of them because she knows that if she witnesses the Head Teacher acting in a way that harms a child or young person then she needs to contact the Chair of Governors. She knows that she can contact the safeguarding governor if she thinks there has been a break down in the safeguarding system. She is pretty sure that she will never need to contact either of them.

Reflective Questions

- Are you clear about the role of the Chair of governors and the safeguarding governor in your school?
- Do you know who both these people are?

The Special Educational Needs and Coordinator (SENCO Sometimes Referred to as SENDCo)

The SENCO is responsible and accountable for the education of all children or young people in the school who are in need of support because of their learning needs. As a result, this person may well take responsibility for some of the children and young people with safeguarding needs. They have usually taken an additional qualification in order to carry out this role.

Children with learning needs or disabilities are more vulnerable to abuse (Powell, Loucks and Trigg, 2007). Needs may also be as a consequence of developmental issues resulting from abuse or neglect (you will see an example of this in case study 7.1 in Chapter Seven). These children will have either a My Plan (meaning that their needs are addressed from within school), a My Plan + (meaning that other agencies are involved in meeting their needs) or and Education Health Care Plan (EHCP – meaning that meeting their needs is complex and set out in a document agreed between the parents, the school and the local authority).

The SENCO is a key person for you to know in school. Make sure that you find out who they are in your first week and introduce yourself to them if you are not scheduled to meet them as part of your induction programme. If there is a particular intervention you would like to develop for a child or young person in your class or one of your classes, then you will need to check if they have a plan and, if they do, whether what you are hoping to do sits comfortably within that. We explore types of early help that you might want to provide in Chapter Nine.

Designated Teacher for Looked After and Previously Looked After Children

This, like the role of DSL and SENCO, is a statutory role. In most schools the role is carried out by someone who holds another role – such as the DSL or the Head Teacher or another member of the SLT. Their role is to ensure that the educational needs of any child or young person who is 'Looked After' or has been 'Looked After' are being met, as this group of children and young people are known to be particularly disadvantaged when it comes to educational achievement (Jackson, Sutcliffe and Smith, 2014). When we talk about 'Looked After' we mean a child or young person who has been taken into care. This is legal process which we will look at briefly in Chapter Two.

Mental Health Lead and Attendance Lead

Depending on the size and make up and needs of your school there may be a mental health lead and/or an attendance lead. Both these roles now have training attached. In some schools these might be the same person and that person might equally be the DSL.

Make sure that you find out if there are any other roles and people that you need to find out about. They will be knowledgeable and will be able to provide support if you find yourself teaching a child or young person with mental health issues or who is regularly absent.

Other Staff Members

This book is particularly aimed at teachers but there are a range of other staff in schools who all have a responsibility for the safeguarding of children and young people.

Teaching assistants are key in safeguarding – they are often the person that children and young people confide in (Bradwell and Bending, 2021). They also are often more free to listen to needs and disclosures. As a class teacher you should work closely with any teaching assistants who are supporting the class or individuals within it to make sure children and young people feel safe and supported. If you are new to a class or a school an experienced teaching assistant is likely to know more about the children or young people, the processes in school and the way to manage safeguarding needs – listen to them and ask for their help and support if needed.

Other support staff are also important as part of the whole school as a safeguarding team. Schools will have a range of other staff members, from caretakers and cleaners to midday supervisors, finance and administrative staff. Everyone has to have the same level of safeguarding training, has to read the safeguarding or child protection policy, along with the code of conduct and part one of *Keeping Children Safe in Education* (DfE, 2024). While they may not take responsibility for a class they are still responsible for keeping children or young people in the school safe and are therefore part of building the safeguarding culture.

Multi-Agency Partners

You may hear this term in your safeguarding training and it appears in figure 1.1 at the beginning of this chapter. What is generally meant by this are the other people who work to keep children or young people safe who do not work for the school. These partners can be people who come into school to support the safeguarding issues that children might experience – for example Educational Psychologists. They might also be from what are referred to as the statutory partners in *Working Together to Safeguard Children* (DfE, 2023 – see Chapter Two) – that is the police, health services or children's social care. They might also be from third sector organisations (charities) who provide support to children or young people and their families. You are unlikely to make referrals to any of these but it is useful to know who they are and in relation to a particular child or young person you may well be asked to provide information so that they can carry out their work. This is where there is often a cross over with children or young people with special educational needs.

Case Study 1.5

Mandy was taken into care when she was in Year One. Her parents were found to have neglected her and her siblings. Among other things all the children slept on the floor. There was often no food in the house, the heating had been disconnected and her Dad had detached the bath from the wall so that the taps did not work.

In Year Two her class teacher noticed that Mandy was becoming withdrawn and not engaging with learning. The class teacher spoke to the DSL who was also the Designated Teacher for Looked After Children. She suggested that some of the money allocated to the school for Mandy could be spent on play therapy to enable her to explore her feelings and perhaps be able to better engage with her learning. The DSL agreed that this would be a good idea and asked the class teacher if she would like to help to complete the referral form.

On the play therapist's first visit he asked to speak to the class teacher to find out how Mandy had been responding in class. After his first session with Mandy he spoke to the class teacher about approaches that might be helpful if Mandy appeared withdrawn in class. This collaborative approach continued for the duration of the play therapist's work.

At the end of the funded sessions Mandy was much more engaged in class, although still sometimes seemed withdrawn. The play therapist spent time with the class teacher suggesting how to continue the support for Mandy so that she could achieve to her full potential despite the neglect that she had been subject to.

Reflective Questions
- How did Mandy's class teacher know something was wrong?
- How did the class teacher and play therapist work together to support Mandy?
- How confident do you feel that you would notice if a child needed support from an external agency? What could you do to find out more?
- What safeguarding issues can you identify?
- How might you apply this case study/learning with the children and young people that you work with?

Other Aspects of Your Role in Safeguarding

In some schools all children or young people are asked to nominate a key adult. Someone who they can talk to if they have worries or concerns; an adult who builds a close professional relationship with that particular child or young person (see Chapter Three). In many schools this happens organically. Again make sure you know what happens in the school that you are working in and make sure that if a child or young person wants you to be their key adult that you spend time getting to know them and that know what the boundaries are.

Finally, many children or young people with safeguarding needs live in poverty (see Chapter Nine). As a result, they might be in receipt of Pupil Premium funding. This is additional money that the school is allocated to support the learning and development of disadvantaged children and young people. You should know if you are teaching children or young people in receipt of this funding and if there is anything particular you should be doing to support them. If you are not sure who they are make sure you ask the Pupil Premium Coordinator if your school has one. Otherwise ask the DSL they will know who the children are and whether the pupil premium is allocated to a child or young person with safeguarding needs.

Document Checklist

For safeguarding you should make sure you read all of these whenever you begin work at a school and re-read them annually:

- *Keeping Children Safe in Education* – Part One (DfE, 2024) (More detail in Chapter Two)
- The school's Safeguarding and or Child Protection Policy
- The school's Staff Code of Conduct
- The school's Allegations Management and Low-Level Concerns Policy (this may be included in the Safeguarding and or Child Protection Policy)
- The school's Behaviour Management or Relationship Policy
- The school's policy for Online Safety

The school will have other policies that they may ask you to read – it might be worth adding an additional question when you meet with the DSL and ask – if there are any other policies they think you should read to enable you to carry out your safeguarding role in the classroom.

Summary for This Chapter

In this chapter, we have looked at the roles and responsibilities of the key people in school who make sure children and young people are kept safe. We started by examining your role in the system providing a simple diagram summarising who is responsible for what. We have then explored the other key roles and how you might interact with them. Finally, there is a document check list that you should read in order to make sure you are well prepared to take on your safeguarding responsibility.

References

Bradwell, M. and Bending, H. (2021) '"I'm just a TA"; From mixing paints to managing safeguarding and class teaching: An exploration of teaching assistant's perceptions of roles in school', *Management in Education*, pp. 1–5.

Department for Education (DfE) (2011) *Teachers' Standards*. London: DfE. Available at: https://assets.publishing.service.gov.uk/media/5a750668ed915d3c7d529cad/Teachers_standard_information.pdf [Accessed 12.11.23].

Department for Education (DfE) (2023) *Working Together to Safeguard Children*. London: DfE. Available at: https://www.gov.uk/government/publications/working-together-to-safeguard-children-2 [Accessed 26.3.24].

Department for Education (DfE) (2024) *Keeping Children Safe in Education*. London: DfE. Available at: https://www.gov.uk/government/publications/keeping-children-safe-in-education-2 [Accessed 26.5.24].

Jackson, S., Sutcliffe, C. R. and Smith, S. J. (2014) 'Educational outcomes of children in care: Understanding the challenges and prioritizing policy options', *British Journal of Social Work*, 44(7).

Powell, H., Loucks, N. and Trigg, W. (2007) 'Abuse and disability: A study into the awareness of support staff in special schools', *British Journal of Learning Disabilites*, 32(3).

2
Knowledge and Understanding of Safeguarding

> **Chapter Aims**
>
> - To introduce the statutory guidance.
> - To explore the knowledge that is required to be effective in your safeguarding practice.
> - To provide examples of what the knowledge might help you recognise in class.

Introduction

This chapter explores the knowledge you need for safeguarding to be an essential part of your classroom safeguarding culture. While it does not replace the need for you to read part one of *Keeping Children Safe in Education* (DfE, 2024) or the school safeguarding policy, it will help you pick your way through these technical documents and help you retain the information that is essential for daily work with children and young people. The Prevent guidance is introduced with a critical analysis of the problems that teachers encounter with it.

Safeguarding Foundations

There are two pieces of guidance in addition to your school policy that underpin safeguarding work in school. While this chapter does not replace the need to read these pieces of guidance, it does provide an accessible summary of what you need to know in order to be excellent in your safeguarding practice.

The first piece of guidance is the statutory *Working Together to Safeguard Children* (DfE, 2023), often referred to as Working Together. This translates the legislation around child protection into what professionals need to do. It also defines safeguarding and the difference between this and child protection.

The main piece of guidance for schools is called *Keeping Children Safe in Education* (DfE, 2024) this is referred to by its initials KCSIE and is often pronounced 'kick-sea'. This is reviewed annually and republished every academic year. In most schools this forms part of the early September induction for all staff because everyone needs to read 'Part One' annually.

Your school will also have its own safeguarding policy (sometimes called the child protection policy) which guides the practice of the staff that work there. It is really important that you are familiar with this as it will detail how to make safeguarding referrals and who you should make those to. More detail about this process is covered in in Chapter Four, while the members of the safeguarding team and your role in it are covered in Chapter One.

Case Study 2.1

In an all through school safeguarding is included during INSET every September. They have introduced a shortened safeguarding policy which has flow charts for the staff to follow and hyperlinks to the NSPCC website definitions for all areas of child abuse and safeguarding issues. They have also produced a summary of *Working Together to Safeguard Children* (DfE, 2023). This means that for safeguarding purposes staff have to read: The policy, Part One of *Keeping Children Safe in Education* (DfE, 2024), the behaviour policy, the staff code of conduct or handbook (as this lays out staff conduct in general) and the summary of Working Together.

Time is given during the INSET for this reading and then staff are asked to complete a Microsoft survey to confirm that they have read and understood the documents. This means that DSL who is the strategic lead for safeguarding, knows that staff have a secure knowledge of safeguarding and child protection in the school.

Reflective Questions

- What is the process in your school for ensuring staff have all the information that they need for safeguarding?
- When you have read all the documents do you have any questions about your safeguarding role? Who can you ask?

What Is Safeguarding and What Is Child Protection?

You will hear both these terms interchangeably but it is useful for you to have clear definitions of both so you know what people are talking about.

Safeguarding is defined in the 2023 version of *Working Together to Safeguard Children* as:

- 'providing help and support to meet the needs of children as soon as problems emerge;

- protecting children from maltreatment, whether that is within or outside the home, including online;
- preventing impairment of children's mental and physical health or development;
- ensuring that children grow up in circumstances consistent with the provision of safe and effective care;
- promoting the upbringing of children with their birth parents, or otherwise their family network through a kinship care arrangement, whenever possible and where this is in the best interests of the children; and
- taking action to enable all children to have the best outcomes in line with the outcomes set out in the Children's Social Care National Framework'.

(DfE, 2023 p7)

Child protection on the other hand is defined by the NSPCC as part of the safeguarding process focusing on protecting individual children identified as suffering or likely to suffer significant harm. Significant harm is the legal term in the *Children Act 1989* (UK Government, 1989) which determines whether a child has been abused – this is covered in the section on key indicators of abuse.

Keeping Children Safe in Education

What then are the key messages from *Keeping Children Safe in Education* (DfE, 2024)? Here we provide an overview and then follow with more detail where this is not covered in other chapters in the book.

The key theme that runs through Part One of the document is that trusted relationships will allow children and young people to communicate what is happening in their lives. You should be aware that children or young people may not always know that they are being abused or be ready to disclose that they are being abused and so their behaviour and presentation in the classroom is more likely to indicate that a child or young person is experiencing challenges. Without the foundation of strong relationships, you will not know the children or young people in your classroom well enough to interpret what is happening – this will be covered in more detail in Chapter Three.

The guidance also goes on to detail what you need to do in order to fulfil your statutory and moral obligations. You should:

- Provide a safe environment for learning (Chapter Eight).
- Know what the key indicators of abuse and neglect are (this chapter).
- Be aware that abuse, neglect and safeguarding are rarely standalone, cannot be covered by one definition or label and in most cases will overlap each other (covered throughout the book).
- Know what to do if a child tells them that they are being abused or neglected (Chapters One and Four).

- Have an awareness of safeguarding issues that can put children at risk of harm (these are included in Annex B of *Keeping Children Safe in Education* and defined later in this chapter).
- Be prepared to identify children who may benefit from early help and know any local process (Chapter Nine).
- Be aware that mental health problems AND behaviour can sometimes be an indicator that a child is suffering or at risk of suffering abuse, neglect and exploitation (Chapter Six).

Keeping Children Safe in Education (DfE, 2024) also details that schools should ensure that teaching safeguarding includes preventative education to 'prepare pupils for modern life'. While most schools will include this as part of the PHSE/RHSE/RSE curriculum– all teachers need to take opportunities to follow up pertinent issues with confidence to help children learn how to keep themselves safe. This will be covered in more detail in Chapter Ten.

In addition, *Keeping Children Safe in Education* (DfE, 2024) has also identified some key areas of safeguarding that all staff need to be aware of and the school needs to do. Schools must ensure that there is a trusted process to prevent and support the identification and management of Child-on-Child abuse including sexual violence and harassment (this is contained in *Keeping Children Safe in Education* Part Five). Your school must also support you to keep children safe online in school and with the issues that they might be facing at home – this is covered in more detail in Chapter Eleven.

Keeping Children Safe in Education (DfE, 2024) also details what to do if you think that another professional is harming or potentially harming a child. This is covered under the allegations management and low-level concerns processes. These are vital to ensure that schools are safe places for children. This will be the focus in the last part of this chapter.

Finally, *Keeping Children Safe in Education* (DfE, 2024) covers the requirement for your training – you should have a clear safeguarding induction in addition to regular update training. You should also complete 'Prevent' training – this will be covered in a later section in this chapter.

The Key Indicators of Abuse

While there are many safeguarding issues that children experience there are specifically four categories in the *Children Act 1989* (UK Government, 1989) – the legislation along with the *Children Act 2004* (UK Government, 2004) that identifies whether a child or young person has suffered or is likely to suffer significant harm.

Physical Abuse

This type of abuse may involve hitting, shaking, throwing, poisoning, burning or scalding, drowning, suffocating or otherwise causing physical harm to a child or young person. It can also be caused when a parent or carer fabricates the symptoms of, or deliberately induces, illness in a child or young person (which you may have heard of by its previous term of Munchausen by proxy but is now called Fabricated and Induced Illness).

Key information for you: It is likely that if you identify that a child or young person has been physically abused that you will see some physical symptoms. Some children, young people and their families, are adept at providing explanations for the 'evidence' you might see. Always speak to the Designated Safeguarding Lead (DSL) or one of the Deputy Designated Safeguarding Leads (DDSLs) if you are concerned that a child or young person is being physically abused. Make sure you do this as early as possible. If a child or young person comes to school with an injury, it may not be safe for them to go home so other members of the safeguarding team will need as much time as possible to act before the end of the school day.

Emotional Abuse

This type of abuse is often difficult to pinpoint but has long-term implications for children and young people. It may involve conveying to a child or young person that they are worthless or unloved, inadequate, or valued only because they meet the needs of another person. It may include not giving the child or young person opportunities to express their views, deliberately silencing them or 'making fun' of what they say or how they communicate. It may feature age or developmentally inappropriate expectations being imposed on children. These may include interactions that are beyond a child or young person's developmental capability as well as overprotection and limitation of exploration and learning or preventing the child or young person from participating in normal social interaction. It may involve seeing or hearing the ill-treatment of another. It may also involve serious bullying (including cyberbullying), causing children or young people frequently to feel frightened or in danger, or their exploitation or corruption. Some level of emotional abuse is involved in all types of child abuse but might also occur on its own.

Key information for you: In order to establish that emotional abuse is happening, you will need to be alert to the lives of the children or young people that you teach. Most children or young people who are being emotionally abused are deeply unhappy – this may manifest itself in various ways (see Chapter Six). Again make sure you speak to the DSL or DDSL if you are concerned. They will help you to record the evidence that is needed to ensure the child or young person gets the help that they need.

Sexual Abuse

This type of abuse, in addition to the damage it causes to children and young people, can be extremely difficult for those who work with the victims. It involves forcing or enticing a child or young person to take part in sexual activities, whether or not the child or young person is aware of what is happening. The activities may involve physical contact, including assault by penetration (for example, rape or oral sex) or non-penetrative acts such as masturbation, kissing, rubbing, and touching outside of clothing. They may also include non-contact activities, such as involving children or young people in looking at, or in the production of, sexual images, watching sexual activities, encouraging children or young people to behave in sexually inappropriate ways, or grooming a child or young person in preparation for abuse. Sexual abuse can take place online, and technology can be used to facilitate offline abuse.

Key information for you: If a child or young person discloses sexual abuse to you or you become aware of a child or young person in your class being a victim of sexual abuse it is vital that you manage your own feelings. The child or young person will need to know that you are not horrified, even if you are. Make sure that you give them space and time to talk if they want to – as with all disclosures or child protection discussions make sure you do not promise to keep anything a secret. This is particularly important for this type of abuse as the child or young person is likely to have been coerced into keeping the adult's behaviour secret. Again make sure you speak to the DSL or DDSL and ask for their support in helping you to manage your own feelings if you find this or any other child abuse issue difficult. No one finds it easy and no one will expect you to 'take it in your stride'.

Neglect

This type of abuse is described simply as the persistent failure to meet a child or young person's basic physical and/or psychological needs, likely to result in the serious impairment of the child or young person's health or development. While this might seem very straight forward it is notoriously difficult to identify and evidence for the purposes of referral to children's social care.

The trajectory of neglect may begin during pregnancy, for example as a result of maternal substance abuse. Once a child is born, neglect may involve a parent or carer failing to: provide adequate food, clothing and shelter (including exclusion from home or abandonment); protect a child or young person from physical and emotional harm or danger; ensure adequate supervision (including the use of inadequate care-givers); or ensure access to appropriate medical care or treatment. It may also include neglect of, or unresponsiveness to, a child or young person's basic emotional needs.

Key information for you: Recording the evidence is key for supporting children or young people who are being neglected. The DSL or DDSL will help you to record this in the format that they need. It is important that you build this from the first observation so that the evidence provides a rich sense of what life is like for the child or young person in your class.

Case Study 2.2

Background
Martha was a six-year-old girl. She lived with both her parents and had two younger siblings. Her mother spoke English as an additional language and was able to understand spoken but not written English. She had been in the school since Reception.

What Happened
It was noticed that Martha had nits, so the class teacher spoke to her Mum and asked her to treat the nits, she recorded this on the school's online safeguarding portal. A week later the class teacher noticed that either the nits had not been removed completely the first time or that they had returned, so she spoke to Martha's Mum again. This time the teacher asked if Mum knew how to get rid of the nits by washing and combing and making sure that all the bedding and clothes had been washed to get rid of any residual eggs, again this was recorded.

Another week passed and the class teacher noticed that not only did Martha have nits again (or again that they had not been removed completely on the previous occasions) but that Martha had scratched so much that she had a sore at the base of her scalp. The class teacher spoke to the DSL about what to do next, in addition to recording what she had witnessed on the school's online safeguarding portal.

The DSL agreed that it was time for him to speak to Mum, which he did with the class teacher present – again explaining how to treat the nits and recommending that Martha be taken to the doctor or pharmacy for some treatment for the sore. He also asked the class teacher to record anything else in relation to Martha so that he could build a picture of her life experiences.

Over the next month the class teacher noticed that Martha had nits on a weekly basis and spoke to Mum about treating every time. She also noticed that Martha's clothes were not being washed as they often had food on them from a previous day or week. When Martha changed for P.E. she could see that Martha had dirt on her wrists and neck. During a Relationships, Health and Sex Education (RHSE) lesson on keeping themselves clean, the children were asked to map how often they had a bath and brushed their teeth. Martha told the teaching assistant that she did not have a toothbrush and that the bath at her house didn't work. After this lesson the class teacher spoke to the DSL again – he agreed that Mum seemed to be struggling to care for Martha so he invited Mum to speak to him at the end of the day. He discussed the concerns, Mum told him that her partner had left and she was struggling at home.

The DSL persuaded Mum to consent to a referral for Early Help for some support with looking after the children. When the Early Help worker went to the house, Mum had changed her mind and refused to let her in. By this time Martha was constantly hungry and asking for food at school so the DSL and the Early Help worker made a joint referral to social care. Martha and her siblings were placed on a child protection

(Continued)

plan and a social worker was appointed to work with the family to improve matters for the children.

Reflective Questions
- What are your thoughts about how long it took to get help for Martha?
- What safeguarding issues can you identify?
- How might you apply this case study/learning with the children and young people that you work with?

Other Areas of Safeguarding

You will learn, throughout your time as a teacher, about a number of other areas of safeguarding or child abuse that are often referred to as safeguarding issues. These are detailed in Annex B of *Keeping Children Safe in Education* and are often defined in detail in safeguarding policies. They include those in the following list – that you can look up in KCSIE when you have time:

- Bullying, including online bullying and prejudice-based bullying.
- Racist, disability and homophobic or transphobic abuse (hate crimes) – See Chapter Eight for how to create a safe space so this does not happen in your classroom.
- Gender-based violence (violence directed against a person because of that person's gender or violence that affects persons of a particular gender disproportionately).
- Child-on-Child/Peer-on-peer abuse such as sexual violence and harassment – You are required to challenge all inappropriate behaviour between children, more about the detail of behaviours that must be challenged are in Part Five of *Keeping Children Safe in Education* (DfE, 2024) and further details are included below.
- Radicalisation and/or extremist behaviour – see below.
- Child sexual exploitation and trafficking – using a child or young person for someone else's advantage, gratification or profit often resulting in unjust, cruel and harmful treatment of the child.
- Child criminal exploitation (where an individual or group takes advantage of an imbalance of power to coerce, control, manipulate or deceive a child or young person) including county lines (where illegal drugs are transported from one area to another, often across police and local authority boundaries, although not exclusively, usually by children or vulnerable young people who are coerced into it by gangs).
- Serious violent crime (covers a variety of offences – ranging from common assault to murder. It also encompasses the use of weapons such as firearms, knives and corrosive substances like acid).
- Online abuse: Knowing the risks linked to using technology and social media, including online bullying; the risks of being groomed online for exploitation or radicalisation and risks of accessing and generating inappropriate content, for

example 'sexting' are an important part of your role (this is covered in more detail in Chapter Eleven).
- Grooming (when a person builds a relationship with a child or young person, so they can abuse them and manipulate them into doing things). Be aware that adults who abuse children and young people often groom the adults around them in order to gain access or to go undetected – this is why the allegations management and low-level concerns process is so important.
- Teenage relationship abuse.
- Upskirting (when someone uses equipment such as a camera or mobile phone to take photos or videos underneath a person's clothes, with the intention of viewing their genitals or buttocks, without their permission).
- Substance misuse.
- Issues that may be specific to a local area or population, for example gang activity or youth violence.
- Domestic Abuse – Children and young people can be victims of domestic abuse in their own right. Experiencing the effects of abuse at home can have a detrimental and long-term impact on health, well-being, development and ability to learn.
- Female genital mutilation (procedures involving partial or total removal of the external female genital organs or any other injury to the female genital organs for non-medical reasons).
- Forced marriage (where one or both people do not, or cannot, consent to the marriage – remember you cannot consent to marriage until you are 18 years old).
- Poor parenting.
- Homelessness.
- So-called honour-based violence (a crime or incident committed to protect or defend the perceived 'honour' of a family or community).

Radicalisation and/or Extremist Behaviour

This safeguarding issue is treated somewhat differently to the others in the above list as all staff in school are required to undertake specific training to prevent radicalisation or extremist behaviour; this is usually referred to as Prevent training.

In order to understand your role, it is important to be clear about the definitions of the behaviour or abuse that we are trying to protect children from:

Extremism is considered to be the holding of extreme political or religious views; fanaticism.
Radicalisation is the process through which a person comes to support or be involved in extremist ideologies.
Terrorism is the unlawful use of violence and intimidation, especially against civilians, in the pursuit of political aims.

As a teacher it is important that you maintain a politically impartial stance so that children and young people can make their own mind up about what they believe in. So preventing children or young people from doing so by stepping in to stop them from developing a particular ideology might seem to be at odds with this. Given the sensitivity of the issues involved, it is important that you understand the messaging and make sure that you view any concerns through a safeguarding lens rather than a political one.

Children or young people who become radicalised to hold extremist views are often 'groomed' by older children, young people or adults who hold these views. These ideologies are generally exclusive requiring complete assimilation without interrogation or acceptance of other opinions. Therein lies the reason for ensuring that children or young people who have been inculcated are supported to broaden their views and prevent them from being further abused in the extremist communities that encourage their involvement. Remember, extremist views can be held at all ends of the political spectrum and are not specific to the particular ideologies that tend to make the popular press.

Case Study 2.3

Background
Ibby lived with his family of three siblings and his Mum. He was the youngest and had fled with his family from war-torn Sudan to refugee camps in Kenya before being settled in the United Kingdom. His uncle had come with the family and sometimes lived with them and sometimes elsewhere.

What happened?
During a Religious Education lesson Ibby told the class that the way Islam was taught was wrong and that they should be learning about martyrs and how to properly live the life that Allah wanted. When the class teacher asked him to be more specific about what he meant, Ibby told her that he did not have to answer her questions as she was a woman and should be at home having babies.

The class teacher spoke to Ibby's Head of Year as part of the pastoral team. He was concerned and asked her to log the behaviour on the safeguarding portal and that he would talk to Ibby. When they had a conversation Ibby talked to the Head of Year about his Uncle and the fact that he had travelled to Pakistan to take part in a camp and was keeping in touch. His Uncle had also sent him some links to websites so that Ibby could learn about 'proper Islam'.

The Head of Year immediately went and had a discussion with the DSL who rang the local police Prevent Officer. The Prevent Officer was familiar with Ibby's uncle but felt that there was no immediate threat and that a safeguarding referral was an appropriate way to proceed.

> **Reflective Questions**
> - Have you completed the prevent training? It can be found here https://www.gov.uk/guidance/prevent-duty-training
> - What safeguarding issues can you identify?
> - How might you apply this case study/learning with the children and young people that you work with?

Child-on-Child/Peer-on-Peer Abuse

This type of abuse warrants particular attention as it has become a key issue in schools of all phases, sexual abuse here is usually referred to as harmful sexual behaviours. All inspection regimes ensure that schools have robust procedures to challenge and report incidents between pupils. Your responsibility is to ensure that the culture in your classroom is such that any issues between the children or young people that you are teaching do not go unnoticed or unchallenged and that they are recorded and followed up. This is particularly important if the behaviours fall under the sexual violence or harassment umbrella. Definitions are contained in Part Five of *Keeping Children Safe in Education* (DfE, 2024) and you need to be aware of what these are – they include legal definitions of rape and sexual assault in addition to behaviours that you are more likely to see in class such as:

- Sexual comments, such as telling sexual stories, making lewd comments, making sexual remarks about clothes and appearance and calling someone by sexualised names.
- Sexual 'jokes' or taunting.
- Physical behaviour, such as deliberately brushing against someone, interfering with someone's clothes. Schools and colleges should be considering when any of this crosses a line into sexual violence – it is important to talk to and consider the experience of the victim.
- Displaying pictures, photos or drawings of a sexual nature.

Make sure you know what the process is in your school and if you are not sure if what you have seen falls into this category make sure you tell the DSL or DDSL to register your concerns.

> ### Case Study 2.4 – Primary
>
> #### Background
> Julius' Mum came into school very distressed and asked to speak to the class teacher. She told him that an older child had asked Julius to go behind the bushes on the edge of the playground and show him 'his willy'. Julius' Mum told the class teacher
>
> *(Continued)*

that this was the second time that it had happened. The class teacher knew that this was an urgent referral to the DSL so asked a child to take a message so that he could to speak to her urgently with the parent.

What Happened?
The DSL spoke to Julius' Mum and was able to identify the older child. The DSL rang the Multi Agency Safeguarding Hub (MASH) team and they advised an investigation before making a referral. The DSL asked the class teacher to make sure that Julius was safe at break time by offering an opportunity to play elsewhere. The DSL also ensured that the older child was not on the playground during the day while further information was gathered. A risk assessment was carried out with regards to the bushes on the edge of the playground, it was decided that they should be cut down.

At the end of the day the class teacher uploaded all the information that had been shared with him on the school safeguarding system.

Reflective Questions
- What safeguarding issues can you identify?
- How might you apply this case study/learning with the children and young people that you work with?

Case Study 2.5 – Secondary

Background
Annie spoke to her form tutor during registration to say that she had been touched on the breast on the bus to school by another member of the year group. Her form tutor knew that she had to act quickly to ensure that there was no further risk to Annie or to others at school so spoke to the DSL straight after registration.

What Happened?
The DSL spoke to Annie and then to the boy who had touched her. He admitted that he had touched her but said it was just as a joke. The DSL explained that touching a female in this way, without consent was never a joke. He contacted both Annie's parents and the parents of the boy. Annie's parents wanted the issue to be referred to the police so this was followed up, in addition to a children's social care referral for the boy. School followed the process they had in place to ensure both Annie and the boy were supported.

The DSL also held a year group meeting to remind the pupils that this sort of behaviour was not a joke and was considered to be sexual assault and could result in serious consequences.

At the end of the day the form tutor uploaded all the information that had been shared with her on the school safeguarding system.

> **Reflective Questions**
> - What safeguarding issues can you identify?
> - How might you apply this case study/learning with the children and young people that you work with?

Contextual Safeguarding

This area of safeguarding is one that is made really clear in *Working Together to Safeguard Children* (2023). In most instances of safeguarding the child or young person is being abused in their home or by a parent or close adult. Contextual safeguarding was first conceptualised by Carlene Firmin (2017) and initially referred to as child-on-child abuse but has now come to be understood as abuse that is experienced outside of the home – that is in the places and spaces that young people, particularly, inhabit where they are vulnerable to abuse.

Other Useful Knowledge

As a student or early career teacher you should not be required manage Child Protection Cases in your school. However, knowing what some of the terminology means will be helpful for your understanding of the safeguarding needs of the children in your class:

Multi Agency Referral Form (MARF) – this is what is completed when the DSL or DDSL feels that the concerns from staff in the school meet the local threshold for referral into child social care (CSC), a department of the Local Authority, and assessment as to whether a child needs a social worker.

Multi Agency Safeguarding Hub (MASH) – most Local Authorities have a filter system for referrals. Many have a MASH where there are representatives from CSC, health, police and education as a minimum. Some have a 'front door'. Whatever it is called this is where the immediate risk to the child is assessed and decisions are made as to what happens next.

Strategy meeting – if there are serious concerns raised about the risk to a child as a result of the MASH assessment, a meeting of all the agencies involved with a child or young person is called so that information can be shared effectively to decide if the child or young person meets the legal definition of being at risk of significant harm.

Section 47 – this is the section of the *Children Act 1989* (UK Government, 1989) that lays out whether a child is at risk of significant harm. If it is agreed at the strategy meeting or through a more thorough assessment that a child is at risk, then an initial Child Protection Conference is held (ICPC). There the professionals and the parents meet and if they feel that the risks meet the criteria the child will be placed on a Child Protection Plan (CP plan). If the professionals feel that a plan is the only way to ensure a child's safety, then the child can be placed on a CP plan with or without the parents' consent. The plan will detail what needs to happen to improve things for the child. Once on a CP Plan there will be a core group of professionals who will meet with the parents, usually monthly, to monitor the progress of the plan. The plan is reviewed at regular intervals at a Review Child Protection Conference (RCPC).

Section 17 – this is the section of the *Children Act 1989* (UK Government, 1989) that details what the criteria are for a child or young person who is in need but not at risk of significant harm. The child or young person in this instance can be placed on a child in need plan (CIN plan). Unlike a CP plan this can only happen with the consent of the parents, to try to improve circumstances for the child or young person. Again there are regular meetings to review the progress of the plan.

Looked After Child (LAC) or Child in Care (CIC) sometimes Child Looked After (CLA) – Sometimes things do not improve significantly despite the work of a child protection plan and through a court process the child will be taken into care. Different local authorities use different terminology. At other times there might be an immediate and urgent risk and social workers will seek an emergency court order or the police (who are the only people who can remove a child from their family without first going to court) will execute their emergency powers to move a child into the care of the local authority where they will be cared for by foster carers while professionals and the courts decide what the long-term plan will be for the child. While they are 'in care' they will have a Personal Education Plan (PEP) which will identify how their emotional and academic progress will be supported. This is often managed by the school's 'Designated Teacher' and the Local Authority's 'Virtual School' who monitor the progress of all children in care and ensure that the additional funding that is available to support children's progress has an impact on improving their outcomes.

Allegations Management and Low-Level Concerns

One of the most difficult things that any teacher has to do is to believe that one of their colleagues or another professional has harmed or has the potential to harm a child or young person. The process that covers this will either be in the school's safeguarding policy or in a separate allegations management and low-level concerns policy. The statement that is often used to underpin allegations management and low-level concerns is 'it could happen here'. Schools with secure safeguarding will encourage all their staff to report anything concerning – no matter who is the cause.

An allegation, in order to be upheld, needs to prove that an adult who works with children or young people is considered to have:

- 'behaved in a way that has harmed a child, or may have harmed a child; and/or
- possibly committed a criminal offence against or related to a child; and/or
- behaved towards a child or children in a way that indicates they may pose a risk of harm to children; and/or
- behaved or may have behaved in a way that indicates they may not be suitable to work with children'.

(DfE, 2024 p92)

Any allegation needs to be referred to the Head Teacher in the first instance, unless it is about the Head Teacher and then it should be referred to the Chair of Governors. They, in turn, must refer the allegation to the Local Authority Designated Officer (LADO). This person (or team of people if you work in a large local authority) will make enquiries as to whether the person against whom the allegation is made has a previous record and will probably require there to be some sort of investigation. This is always difficult for all those involved so it is important that if you have made the allegation you have support (potentially from a senior colleague or your union). If an allegation is made against you the school should appoint someone to liaise with you and you should also inform your union as they will be able to support you through any investigation.

Alongside any of the process with regards to the adults involved, if an adult is alleged to have harmed a child or young person in the school the DSL should take a lead role in ensuring that the child or young person is now safe and any referrals that they might need have been made. If you are the first witness to an incident where one of your colleagues has harmed a child or young person – your first responsibility is ensuring that the child or young person is safe and then that the DSL has been informed. If you think that the adult is a risk to other children or young people in the school then you will need to urgently engage other colleagues, without causing panic or hysteria to make sure that children or young people are safe. In reality this is likely to be very rare; however, you should be aware of your responsibilities just in case.

What is more likely is that you may come across colleagues about whom you have an uncomfortable feeling in terms of their interactions with children or young people. Since the 2021 edition of *Keeping Children Safe in Education*, this has been covered by the low-level concerns process. A low-level concern behaviour is one that is inconsistent with the staff code of conduct, including inappropriate conduct outside of work; and does not meet the allegations threshold or is otherwise not considered serious enough to consider a referral to the LADO. Some of the examples that are given to support you in thinking about whether you need to report a low-level concern behaviours are:

- 'being over friendly with children;
- having favourites;
- taking photographs of children on their mobile phone;
- engaging with a child on a one-to-one basis in a secluded area or behind a closed door; or
- humiliating pupils'.

(DfE, 2024 p107)

It is not only important that you recognise these in others but that you make sure that you do not behave in this way yourself.

Case Study 2.6

Background
Andrew was a student teacher on placement in a local secondary school. At the bottom of a stairwell he saw a female teacher and a Year 9 boy. He wasn't sure what they were doing but there was no one else around and the boy was in the corner with the teacher front of him, close enough to touch.

What happened?
What he had seen made Andrew feel uncomfortable so he went to the Head Teacher and told her what he had seen. She thanked him and said that she would take it from there. Andrew was not informed of what else happened but he knows that the teacher involved no longer works at the school.

Reflective Questions
- If this makes you feel uncomfortable who can you talk to, to help you work through the professional challenges in this area?
- What safeguarding issues can you identify?
- How might you apply this case study/learning with the children and young people that you work with?

Summary for This Chapter

In this chapter, we have explored the knowledge contained in the statutory guidance that you need to know in order to keep children and young safe in your classroom. The key messages from *Keeping Children Safe in Education* (DfE, 2024) have been explored. More detail has been provided about the four types of child abuse followed by a list of other safeguarding issues with brief definitions that readers can follow up for themselves. More information has also been provided about the Prevent Duty and why it might be controversial for teachers. You have been provided with a brief summary of terminology that is used in the child protection/safeguarding arena so that you are aware of what the status of some of the children in your class means. Finally, an explanation of the difficult area of Allegations Management and Low-Level concerns including who you can seek support from both if you have to make and allegation or if an allegation or low-level concern is aimed at you.

References

Department for Education (DfE) (2023) *Working Together to Safeguard Children*. London: DfE. Available at: https://assets.publishing.service.gov.uk/media/65cb4349a7ded0000c79e4e1/Working_together_to_safeguard_children_2023_-_statutory_guidance.pdf [Accessed 16.2.24].

Department for Education (DfE) (2024) *Keeping Children Safe in Education*. London: DfE. Available at: https://www.gov.uk/government/publications/keeping-children-safe-in-education-2 [Accessed 26.5.24].

Firmin, C. (2017) 'Contextual risk, individualised responses: An assessment of safeguarding responses to nine cases of peer-on-peer abuse', *Child Abuse Review*, 27, pp. 42–57.

UK Government (1989) *Children Act 1989, c. 41*. London: HMSO. Available at: www.legislation.gov.uk/ukpga/1989/41/contents [Accessed 26.3.24].

UK Government (2004) *Children Act 2004, c. 31*. London: HMSO. Available at: www.legislation.gov.uk/ukpga/2004/31/contents [Accessed 26.3.24].

3

Building Relationships as a Foundation for Safeguarding

> **Chapter Aims**
>
> - To understand why relationships are important in safeguarding.
> - To develop strategies for developing relationships in the classroom.
> - To think about whom to develop these relationships with.
> - To develop strategies for managing difficult relationships.
> - To understand the limits of professional relationships.

Introduction

This chapter explores the relationships between children, young people and staff, between staff and staff and between staff and the children or young people's parents presenting how they are the foundation of safeguarding culture. It sets out why and how relationships, trust, professional love and communication ensure that abuse and trauma is found and prevented. Here we will be focusing on how teachers develop the positive relationships that enable children and young people to feel safe and secure and therefore share their experiences and feelings while creating a safe environment will be covered later on in Chapter Eight.

Why Positive Relationships?

Brummer (2020 p14) says that 'relationships matter in the classroom'. If we are to reach children and young people at any level we need to think about why and how these are created.

If we look at Maslow's 'Hierarchy of Needs', we see that the need for love and belonging sits in the middle (see Figure 3.1). We will look at the rest of the pyramid in more detail in Chapter Seven; however, the need for love is key in talking about relationships. In his book *Maslow before Bloom* (2020), Dr Bryan Pearlman describes how the needs that children and young people have should be addressed before they can access the academic curriculum and learn. This is particularly relevant for those children and young people who are experiencing safeguarding issues (abuse or trauma) as they are less likely to have their needs met by parents or at home. Olson and Cozolino (2014) also describe how 'a classroom is far more than a room of separate individuals; it is a web of interconnected relationships' (preface). It is essential, then, for teachers to understand how to build positive relationships that can enable all children and young people and specifically those who have a deficit to flourish and thrive.

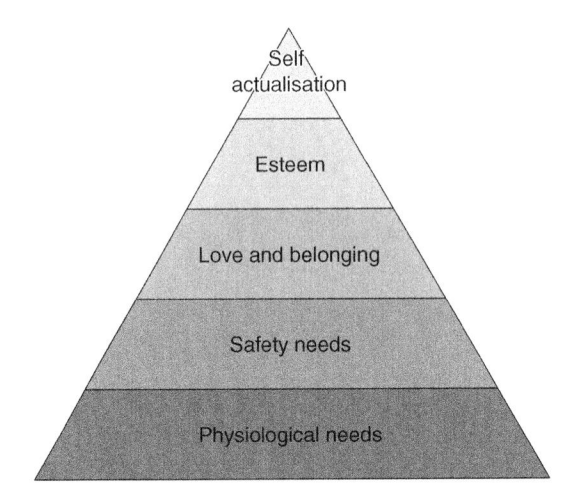

Figure 3.1 Maslow's Hierarchy of Needs (after Maslow, 1943)

In some schools the Behaviour Management Policy has been rewritten as a Relationship Policy. We will look more closely at behaviour in Chapter Six; however, here it is important to note that when you chose to work in a school these policies should reflect your approach to relationships with the children, young people and the colleagues that you work with. So, make sure you explore a school's policies and practices before you accept a job. Some schools, for example will have a policy about touching pupils – it is important to make sure that you understand the remit of your professional practice in this respect; however, if you are a 'natural hugger' (Ferguson, Kelly and Pink, 2022 p13) then working in a school where professional touch is forbidden might be a challenge. In schools where professional touch is allowed or even encouraged the safeguarding culture should be one of ensuring that the child or young is happy to give permission to receive that touch, children and young people are taught to ask adults if they need a hug – essential for learning consent – and should never be behind closed doors.

What Are Positive Relationships?

There are a multitude of definitions of what a positive relationship is. You only have to ask any online search engine and you will see for yourself. Despite this proliferation – if you look closely you will find that there are some words that come up time and again and it is these that will underpin what we are going to explore in this chapter and they have been used to develop the model in Figure 3.2. Before this it is important to remember that adults need to smile at children and young people. When we smile it shows that we are willing to have a positive interaction, it is the beginning of relationship and it opens the door to all that is discussed in this chapter.

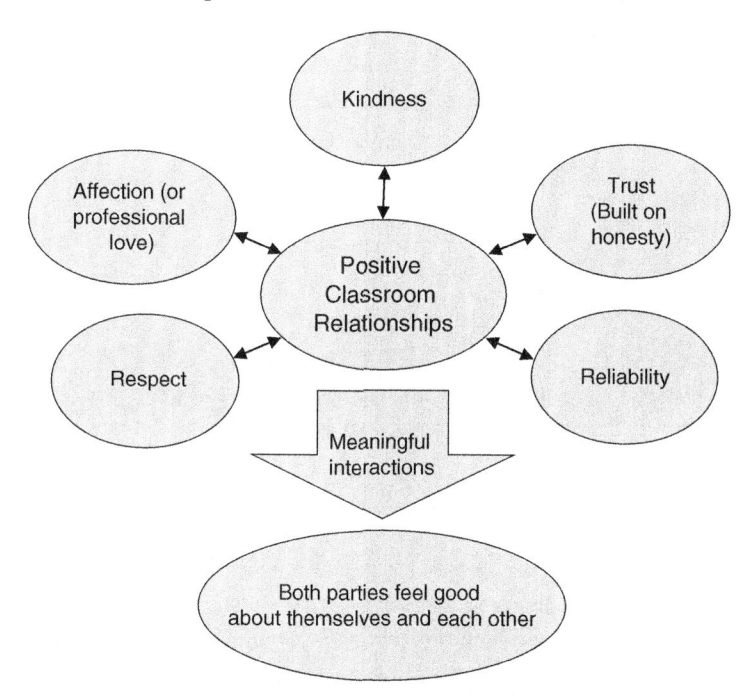

Figure 3.2 A Model of Positive Relationships in the Classroom

How to Develop Positive Relationships in the Classroom to Support Safeguarding

Taking the model of positive relationships in Figure 3.2 – let's look at how you might develop each of the aspects and why they are relevant to safeguarding.

Affection or Professional Love

We rarely talk about love in the teaching profession. We talk about liking children and young people or being passionate about making a difference for them. Dr Jools Page (2018) describes professional love as being 'situated' in the place of work and in the 'complex lives' of the children and young people that we care for. She places professional love in the context of attachment theory (which we will explore more in Chapters Six and Seven), suggesting that as professionals in education the love we show our pupils compliments or even substitutes for the love that is received or not received at home (Page, 2018). Not only that 'human brains are wired to learn best within the context of a loving relationship' (Olson & Cozolino, 2014 preface) so relationships with all children and young people are vital for learning too.

Why Is This Relevant to Safeguarding?

Given that many of the children and young people you will come across in your career may be suffering from emotional abuse or neglect (see Chapter Two) we can begin to see why part of your safeguarding role is to ensure that children and young people have positive relationships with adults in school where they are genuinely held in high regard. This is professional love. Michelle Obama, in her book *The Light We Carry* (2022), is one of a number of people who describe how the influence of this professional love can make a difference. She recalls the 'warmth she felt from her third-grade teacher' describing her as 'lighting up for her' (p82).

> ### Reflective Questions
>
> Think about your own education:
> - Who lit up for you?
> - What were the relationships like with those teachers that **you** loved?
> - What did they do that you can emulate in your relationship building with children?

Kindness

In thinking about kindness, *The Boy, the Mole, the Fox and the Horse* comes to mind (Mackesy, 2019). The book is a great source of ideas about love, life, challenges and kindness saying that 'Nothing beats kindness...it sits quietly beyond all things' (n.p.). We can all think about times when we have received and, conversely, not received kindness and how those things made us feel. Imagine now that you are a child or young person where home is confusing or frightening who learns in a classroom where the teacher is not kind, all the time. The child or young person is likely to respond to that lack of kindness or the surety that kindness will be there by being less positive about the learning. This is true whatever the age of the child or young person irrespective of whether they might be adolescent and full of hormones which means they may be unable to reciprocate that kindness.

Why Is This Relevant to Safeguarding?

For children and young people who have experienced abuse, trauma or have safeguarding issues kindness is the easiest of gifts to give. Consistent kindness at school or in a particular lesson provides a kind of sanctuary where they can be sure of the positivity of the relationships therein. Kindness is the first step in the movement towards building trust.

Trust

Trust is described in the Oxford dictionary as the 'firm belief in the reliability, truth or ability of someone'. For children and young people to trust teachers they need to be sure that that teacher will respond positively and that they will keep their word. If you are able care for children and young people well and consistently you will enable them to develop trust in you that supports the positive relationship you are creating between you. If at all possible it is important for this trust to be reciprocal. Even when children and young people are unreliable, which they often are due to their developmental stage or the abuse they have received, you showing trust in them will further enable them to develop trust in you.

This trustworthiness, defined as 'the ability to be relied on as honest or truthful' is a key aspect of a trauma informed approach (see Chapter Seven). For those who have experienced abuse or trauma, life can be a scary place. For children and young people, trustworthiness means always knowing that adults in school are going to do what they say they are going to do. One way this can be done is by not making promises. If a child or young person asks an adult to do something for them, that adult saying that they will try their best or do what they can, is an honest and truthful answer. Combined with explaining that they cannot promise because there are other factors which might prevent it from happening helps a child or young person understand reliability. The same goes for if an adult is unsure about an answer if a child or young person asks a question. Over time these responses show children and young people that the adults in school are reliable. It is from this that trust is built.

Why Is This Relevant to Safeguarding?

Children and young people with safeguarding, trauma and safeguarding needs have a great need for trusted adults around them. You will often hear this in safeguarding training and you will read about it in *Keeping Children Safe in Education* (DfE, 2024). Having trusted adults around them means that children and young people are more likely to disclose their circumstances at home or in other aspects of their lives. They are more likely to do this because they know that the trusted adult will do something about what they are told (see Chapter Four) and will respond with kindness and professional love.

Respect

In an ideal world we would have mutual respect at all times in our classrooms. In reality there are times when the children and young people we work with are not able to afford us the respect that we would like to see. We however should always show respect and expect it in return. Building on trust – respect is about affording regard for others' feelings and wishes including their rights.

Why Is This Relevant to Safeguarding?

A child or young person is unlikely to disclose their experiences if they think that a teacher will not show respect for how they are feeling (this links to feeling ashamed as explored in Chapter Seven). Children and young people who need to talk to adults in school are also unlikely to do so if they think there will be no respect for what they want to happen. While this is difficult in terms of making sure a child or young person is kept safe, if you work in a respectful way with the child's rights at the heart of what you do then you will be able to negotiate this effectively. One way to do this is never to promise to keep anything that is said a secret and always discuss with the child or young person what you will do next if they have confided in you. Practise what you will say so that you sound confident and competent when a disclosure is made, more of this in Chapter Four.

Reliability

If we think about the relationships that we most cherish, they are the ones where the other person is consistently there for us, no matter what. Children and young people need this in their relationships too. Building on trust and respect, reliability affords children and young people the security that they need in Maslow's 'Safety needs' (see Figure 3.1). Reliability in school can often be seen in boundaries that are created to enable children and young people to feel safe. It can also be created through relationship – knowing who you are what they can expect of you gives children and young people that security that you are reliable and won't let them down.

Why Is This Relevant to Safeguarding?

When other adults in their lives have let them down – having a trusted, reliable adult at school who is kind and shows professional love enables a child to feel secure and loved is vital to replace their needs for attachment (Chapters Six and Seven). This meets those basic needs that have not been met, ensures that support is put in place through referrals to others in school or other agencies (see Chapter Four) and ultimately ensures that a child is in a better position to access learning.

> ### Reflective Questions
>
> Think about all these aspects of relationship:
>
> - What do you most value in your own relationships?
> - What do you think your relationships with the children and young people you work with should look like?
> - How do you think you will create these relationships?

If we build positive relationships, then we will enable meaningful interactions in the classroom. Harmut Rosa (2019), a sociologist who explores what it is to live a good life, describes how the curriculum should be subordinate to positive relationships. He talks about creating 'resonance' where in the classroom there are 'vibrating resonant wires' which enable the teacher to meet children and young people where they are, cultivating relationships which ultimately lead to the development of a positive relationship with the world (Rosa, 2019 p240). If we are able to do this we will, most of the time, feel good about ourselves and as a consequence the children and young people in our care will feel good about themselves and so will thrive in our care irrespective of what they are experiencing at home.

Self-Worth

Children and young people who have experienced abuse, trauma or safeguarding issues are highly likely to feel bad about themselves. They may have been emotionally abused and as a result have been convinced of the nasty things that have been said about and to them. They may have been told that the physical or sexual abuse is as a result of them being inadequate or bad. They may have made a disclosure that has led to difficulties in the family that they have been or feel blamed for. They may have been diagnosed formally or informally with mental health conditions or disorders such as attachment disorder. All of these experiences are likely to have a negative impact on the developing identity of the child or young person causing them to internalise a deficit of self-worth.

Add to this the fact that being a child or young person is likely to place them in a position of feeling powerless meaning that children and young people who have been abused or traumatised are likely to be cautious of relationships and the power differential therein. Rachel Burr (2022) in her book *Self-Worth in Children and Young People* describes how

> Adults still hold the driving seat, and we still do not always adequately listen to children or always actively respond to this and other people's concerns when their well-being is under threat. (Burr, 2022 p9)

She then says

> if we are properly listened to, cared for and treated with love and kindness, then we are likely to develop positive self-worth and have the mental space to enjoy going about our daily lives feeling secure enough to be interested in the wider work and open to new experiences. (Burr, 2022 p20)

Given this, it is clear how positive relationships can intervene to improve how a child or young person feels about themselves and therefore their ability to develop the resilience or fortitude needed to persevere in their learning. It is vital that we begin by 'accepting students for who they are in a given moment' (Olson & Cozolino, 2014 p6) and progress from there helping children and young people to develop a secure understanding of their own worth through our valuing of them.

Case Study 3.1

Background

Sarah lived with her extended family in an area described as being of high deprivation. The house was crowded and she and her siblings slept on the floor as there was no money for beds for them in the small bedroom that they shared with their

(Continued)

mother. She had no private space as her many uncles, aunts and cousins were always in the communal areas of the house.

What Happened?
At school, Sarah was a well behaved little girl who quietly got on with her work, although she often found it hard. One morning as the other children and young people were going out to break she asked the class teacher if she could sit quietly in the book corner and read. This was not normally allowed but the teacher knew that she could trust Sarah to be sensible and she was going to be in and out of the classroom preparing for the next lesson. This pattern continued over the rest of the academic year. Whenever the teacher could she allowed Sarah to read, often recommending books and finding them in the school library or other classrooms for her. Sarah thrived as a result of this respect and kindness and worked hard in her lessons growing academically. When Sarah moved on to the next year group she continued to come back to the teacher with whom she had built such a positive relationship to read at break and lunchtimes whenever she could. One day Sarah asked if she could talk to the teacher – she told her about sleeping on the floor at home and asked if the teacher could help. The teacher spoke to the Designated Safeguarding Lead (DSL) and after a conversation with Sarah's mum made a referral to Early Help at the local authority to support with finding a house for the family to live in.

Sarah went on to secondary school but would occasionally come back and speak to the teacher. When she left secondary school she returned to her primary school for a Teaching Assistant apprenticeship. The teacher encouraged her and with that belief in herself Sarah undertook an access course, went to university and then on to teacher training herself.

She tells how the relationship with this teacher was what led her to believe that she could achieve. The safeguarding support being almost entirely wrapped up in the trust, kindness and professional love provided by the teacher.

Reflective Questions
The teacher built the relationship based on Sarah's needs, initially by giving her a safe space at break time. She showed trust in Sarah and this was reciprocated – the rapport that was built meant that eventually Sarah felt that she could rely on the teacher to respond to her other needs and support her in both her personal and academic life.

- What do you think the safeguarding issues were here?
- How might you apply this case study/learning with the children and young people that you work with?

Who Does a Class Teacher Have Relationships With?

Children
The primary relationship for all teachers is with the children and young people they work with day to day, followed by other children and young people in the school.

With this in mind it is important to build those relationships carefully with the aspects of relationship we have explored in this chapter. It should go without saying that the only way to build these positive relationships is by knowing your children or young people really well. Make the time to find out about them – what do they like, what are they interested in, what is their background and what makes them tick? This will enable you to establish their needs and how you need to be in the relationship with them. This will be key when we explore their behaviour (Chapter Six) and their trauma, shame, Adverse Childhood Experiences (ACEs) and attachment needs (Chapter Seven). Some schools have a system whereby children and young people can identify a key adult. If this is the case and you are nominated by one or more pupils – make sure you take the time to get to know them especially well.

Remember children and young people who have experienced abuse, trauma or safeguarding issues often find relationships difficult and even once they are established often behave in ways that are unlovable in an attempt to break the connections that you build. If you have a child or young person who does this try not to take it personally (use the well-being strategies in Chapter Five). Also make sure you give the child or young person opportunities to repair – teaching them how to do this without shame (Chapters Six and Seven).

Other Staff

Professional relationships with other members of staff are important for a number of reasons, not least of which because they are all part of the safeguarding team, as we discussed in Chapter One. In some schools all the staff like each other and get along well. In others the staff are able to work professionally together despite their differences. In most schools there is a combination of those who actively like each other and those who work together professionally. In a very few schools the relationships between the adults are toxic – where undermining and bullying behaviour is rife. If you find yourself in a school like this make sure you seek the support of your union with the ultimate goal of moving to a school where relationships between the adults are less difficult. The relationships between adults serve as a model to the children and young people in the school. They also create the culture that enables children and young people to flourish and thrive. Without positive or at the very least professional relationships in a school, children and young people who have experienced abuse, trauma or who have safeguarding needs will not feel safe enough to have their needs met and therefore access learning.

Parents or Carers

You will also have a relationship with the parent(s) or carer(s) of the children and young people you teach irrespective of the age and phase of children and young people you teach. How you manage these relationships will be different; however, the model for how you develop positive relationships still applies. Relationships with parent(s) or carer(s) are vital for safeguarding and can be the difference between change happening for a child and change not happening. As the child or young person's teacher you are, particularly if you are *the* teacher that the child or young person has a positive relationship with, likely to be the person at school in whom the parent(s) or carer(s) have the most confidence. Treat this relationship with care – you could be pivotal in ensuring that a family engages with support and enables their child or young person to flourish and thrive in your classroom,

Case Study 3.2

Background

Fred's Design Technology (D.T.) teacher had built a good relationship with Fred and also his Dad. As a result, there had been a couple of times when other teachers had asked the D.T. teacher to ring Dad to remind him of forms that needed to be completed or equipment that Fred needed to bring to school. As he moved into GCSE Fred had chosen D.T. and the relationship between the teacher and Fred's Dad continued to develop over support for the significant amount of coursework which Fred was finding difficult.

What Happened?

A number of teachers had noticed that not only was Fred struggling with course content but that he was appearing unwashed and in clothes that were not clean. The caretaker had even found Fred stealing food from another pupil's bag. The concerns had been reported to the DSL who had agreed to speak to Fred's Dad. The DSL decided to speak to the D.T. teacher as she knew they had a good relationship. The D.T. teacher felt confident to speak to Dad and gave him a call. He told Dad that the school was a bit worried and explained the concerns. He asked if there was anything wrong and could school do anything to help. Dad was initially indignant that it was being suggested that he was not caring for Fred but with the D.T. teacher remaining calm – reminding Dad that he really cared about Fred and wanted to help like he had done with the coursework Dad finally admitted that he was struggling to manage everything at home for Fred and his younger sister as he had to take on extra shifts to be able to pay all the bills.

The DSL was able to arrange for some Early Help support for the family (see Chapter Nine) and liaised with the primary school for Fred's younger sister so that they could support too.

Reflective Questions
- How did a good relationship help facilitate change for Fred?
- What do you think the safeguarding issues are?
- How might you apply this case study/learning with the children and young people that you work with?

Other Professionals

In the early part of your career you may have little interaction with professionals from other agencies – like those we talked about in Chapter One. It is important that when you do get to work with these individuals that you use your positive relationship skills to support the safeguarding of the children and young people that you teach.

Other Members of the Local Community

Again, in the early part of your career you may have little interaction with other members of the local community. However, it is important that you understand the context of your school. What is the local community like – is it a safe place for the children or young people that you teach? Who are the key safe adults in the community and how do they interact with the school? Many schools are embedded in the life of the community that they serve. If this is the case make sure that you get involved. The children and young people that you teach will see that you are interested in their lives outside the classroom and this will support you to build relationships with them.

Case Study 3.3

Background

Anna was a parent of three children and young people in the school. She had separated from their father as a result of domestic abuse and was working long hours to support the family financially. The eldest child's behaviour was beginning to deteriorate and the secondary school which she attended was beginning to be concerned about her and whether she would be able to sit her GCSEs. The other children and young people were still in primary school.

What Happened

The eldest child's form tutor raised the falling attendance with the DSL as it had coincided with a change in behaviour and she was worried. The DSL contacted the siblings' school to see if there was a problem with the younger children. The DSL at the primary school did not know the children and young people or Anna well but knew that the class teacher of the youngest child often spoke to Anna when she collected him from school and offered for the class teacher to speak to Anna about her eldest daughter.

The two DSLs briefed the class teacher about what to say, articulating why the reducing attendance was a concern and also a risk to her daughter but also encouraging Anna by telling her how this was not a criticism of her parenting which both schools had always found to be positive. They asked the class teacher to suggest a meeting with the secondary school. While the class teacher was new to teaching he knew Anna reasonably well and had built a relationship with her over the first term through showing kindness and respect.

(Continued)

He spoke to Anna who was shocked that her eldest daughter was not at school. She asked the class teacher to sit in with her when she attended the meeting with the secondary school which the primary school offered to host so that Anna felt as comfortable as she could. The meeting was attended by Anna, the eldest child's form tutor, the two DSLs and the youngest child's class teacher who was there to act as 'professional friend' for Anna. They discussed the changes in behaviour and the reducing attendance, the risks and what they could all do about it. A plan was put in place which included the form tutor and the teacher of the youngest child being nominated to support Anna while she tried to improve things for her daughter.

While her eldest child still struggled to access learning her attendance improved, with Anna and the staff from both school able to protect her from the risks she had been exposing herself to.

Reflective Questions
- Referring back to Chapter Two – what do you think the risks were to Anna's eldest daughter when she was not attending school?
- Think about the relationships Anna had and those that she built in order to protect her daughter? What do you think the teachers (both primary and secondary) did to build the relationships with Anna?
- This is a good example of how schools can work together, while this is often done by other members of the safeguarding team – think about what your role could be, particularly where your pupils have siblings. Do you know about the family of the children and young people in your class? Do they know about yours? How would this help you build relationships?
- How might you apply this case study/learning with the children and young people that you work with?

Managing Difficult Relationships

At some point in your career as a teacher you will experience at least one difficult relationship. It is useful to think this through before it happens so that you have strategies to help both you and the other person when this happens. When the difficult relationship is with a child that you teach it makes all the elements we have discussed in this chapter really difficult to achieve.

The first thing to do is accept that you will not like all the children and young people (or adults) you work with during your career. This is not a personality fault so do not think badly of yourself when it happens – if you do this will only make the need for an ongoing relationship with the child or colleague more difficult.

You then need to think about the elements of the relationship module in figure 3.2 and work out how you can show them even if you are struggling or they are, to build a positive relationship. Ultimately this can be summarised as 'always be kind' and this includes to yourself. If you can be kind, then you may well be able to build the respect and trust needed to move forward in this particular relationship. Don't be afraid to ask for help to ensure that others are supporting you with any relationship you find difficult.

> ### Case Study 3.4
>
> ### Background
> Leanne had been in netball club for two years. Despite her best efforts the teacher who coached the netball team had found it really difficult to gel with Leanne. She understood that Leanne was quite a clingy child because of the abuse she had received and even though she was now in care Leanne still had attachment difficulties which made it difficult for her to leave the teacher's side. (See Chapter Seven.) This made netball practice quite difficult.
>
> ### What Happened?
> The netball teacher decided to face this head on and ask Leanne what she needed to be able to take part in practice without being glued to her side. She spent time chatting to Leanne at break times when she was on duty and talked to her about the need to find space in a netball match.
>
> Gradually over time Leanne became more confident to move away from the teacher during practice. The more time the teacher spent with Leanne at break time the better this got.
>
> ### Reflective Questions
> - How did the teacher build a relationship with Leanne?
> - What do you think the safeguarding issues are?
> - How might you apply this case study/learning with the children and young people that you work with?

Difficult relationships also tend to be those where having conversations are tricky. The key to managing these is, in the first instance, to tackle them rather than dodge them and we will cover this in Chapter Four. There may also be times where you have to, carefully, extricate yourself from colleague relationships. You should never have developed relationships with children, young people or their parents that become this uncomfortable. Seek support if relationships with colleagues turn sour working out who you can trust to make sure you keep yourself safe.

Limits of Professional Relationships

In this chapter, we have explored how to build the positive relationships that are needed to keep children and young people safe. We have even talked about professional love. It is important, though, to remember that all these relationships are developed in your professional role and therefore should be boundaried. In Chapter Four we will look at how you ensure your social media is kept private and in Chapter Eleven we will look at online interactions more holistically. Here, there is a case study which shows what can happen when you do not keep the boundaries between you and the children and young people you work with on a professional footing.

Case Study 3.5

Background
In the school that Jeremy worked in staff were all called by either Mr, Mrs or Miss and then their surname. This was something that Jeremy was familiar with from his own schooling so it did not seem unusual. The school encouraged staff to build relationships with the children and young people in their classes in order to help them feel safe and happy in school and therefore promote a positive learning environment. When Jeremy started working with the lower sixth he was pleased to see that there was a young person in his class who he knew of from the rugby club. He made sure to greet her warmly the first time he saw her and was surprised that she seemed a bit awkward.

What Happened?
The following weekend when Jeremy saw the young person at the rugby club he made sure to speak to her and ask if everything was all right as she had been a bit off in his lesson the previous week. She told him he was being weird and he said that as he was her teacher she should be a bit nicer to him. He was then called by his friends at the bar and he didn't think any more of it.

After school on Monday Jeremy was called in to see the Head Teacher. He said he had received a complaint from a young person in one of his classes who said that he had approached her outside of school in a way that had made her feel uncomfortable and that he was investigating this as a low-level concern.

Reflective Questions
- What do you think happened here to cause Jeremy to face a Low-Level Concern investigation?
- In your role as a teacher how do you think you should maintain professional boundaries with children or young people outside of school, even if you have met them in social settings before your relationship with them as a teacher?
- How do you think you can protect yourself from any accusations of being unprofessional with children or young people that you know well, for example as relatives or children of friends?
- How might you apply this case study/learning with the children and young people that you work with?

Summary for This Chapter

In this chapter, we have thought about building relationships with the children and young people in our school as well as their parents and our colleagues. We have also explored what we might do when relationships are difficult. What we do to ensure that we keep relationships at school on a professional footing, albeit making sure that we show professional love to the children and young people we teach so that we can keep them safe.

References

Brummer, J. (2020) *Building a Trauma-Informed Restorative School: Skills and Approaches for Improving Culture and Behavior*, London: Jessica Kingsley Publishers.

Burr, R. (2022) *Self-Worth in Children and Young People*. Plymouth: Critical Publishing.

Department for Education (DfE) (2024) *Keeping Children Safe in Education*. London: DfE Available at: https://www.gov.uk/government/publications/keeping-children-safe-in-education–2 [Accessed 26.5.24]

Ferguson, H., Kelly, L. and Pink, S. (2022) 'Social work and child protection for a post-pandemic world: The re-making of practice during COVID-19 and its renewal beyond it', *Journal of Social Work Practice*, 36(12), pp. 5–24.

Mackesy, C. (2019) *The Boy, the Mole, the Fox and the Horse*. London: Ebury.

Maslow, A. H. (1943) 'A theory of human motivation', *Psychological Review*, 50(4), pp. 430–437.

Obama, M. (2022) *The Light We Carry*. New York: Viking.

Olson, K. and Cozolino, L. (2014) *The Invisible Classroom*. New York: W. W. Norton & Company.

Page, J. (2018) 'Characterising the principles of professional love in early childhood care and education', *International Journal of Early Years Education*, 26(2), pp. 125–141.

Pearlman, B. (2020) *Maslow before Bloom: Basic Human Needs before Academics*. Amazon/KDP.

Rosa, H. (2019) *Resonance A Sociology of Our Relationship to the World*. Cambridge: Polity Press.

4

Safeguarding Communication

> **Chapter Aims**
>
> - To understand how to manage conversations with children and young people about abuse and trauma and how these should be recorded.
> - To explore techniques for having difficult conversations with children or young people, their parents, colleagues and other professionals.
> - To think about how records should be written and how to adhere to data protection guidance.
> - To think about how to maintain professional communication especially in relation to digital and social media.

Introduction

This chapter looks at the specifics of how to communicate with others about safeguarding. It includes how to record concerns, how to speak to children and young people and how and when to speak to their parents and how to keep this information safe. You will be able to develop their ability to have difficult conversations that have a lasting impact on the lives of the children and young people in their care.

It will also cover how to maintain a professional relationship through communication with children, young people and their families, particularly in relation to social media use.

Talking to Children and Young People

If a child or young person is experiencing abuse or trauma and choses to tell you about it this can be one of the most challenging conversations you will ever have. You will feel a whole range of emotions when this happens and the key to keeping that child or young person safe will be, in the first instance, by managing your own feelings and emotions. We talk in Chapter Five about how you look after your well-being in order to support both your own emotions and the well-being of children in a more general sense. Here we will discuss how, in the moment, you can hold onto your feelings so that you can support the child or young person who is talking to you and what you need to do afterwards both for them and for yourself.

Hearing a Disclosure

When a child or young person tells you what is happening to them we call this a 'disclosure'. You need to be able to be fully present during a disclosure so that you can really listen to what is being said and so that you can say the right things in response. Later in this section there is a diagram (Figure 4.1) which will help you with the process you have to follow, knowing what you have to do is the first thing that will help when a child or young person choses to disclose to you.

Secondly, knowing what sorts of things can happen to children and young people so that you are not overly shocked by what they are saying will help you manage your feelings and your reactions. While much of the abuse, neglect and trauma that children and young people experience is shocking it is important not to reveal that this is what you think when they tell you about them. While you should not be immune to the horror of what sometimes happens to children and young people you do need to manage disclosures calmly. One way to do this is to be familiar with the sorts of things that you might hear is to know about the sorts of abuse, neglect and trauma that children and young people experience by reading books like this that have case studies in to illustrate the types of abuse that are detailed in the statutory guidance *Keeping Children Safe in Education* (DfE, 2024) and the school policy. You can also look for case studies, serious case reviews or ask colleagues about their experiences, anonymised of course, to broaden your experience of hearing real-life narratives.

In addition to knowing what to do and what sorts of issues you might hear make sure that you have rehearsed what you will do. When our heart rate rises, which yours will do when a child or young person discloses, we are in danger of entering survival mode, not least of which because we are likely to panic slightly when in this situation. This is where our basic instincts kick in and we are not able to use the thinking part of our brain, we discuss this in more detail in relation to children and young people in Chapters Six and Seven. If you disconnect when a child or young person discloses you will not be able to do what you need to do *unless* you have practised it to such a degree that it has become an automatic behaviour. Being able to move effortlessly into what you need to do because you have rehearsed it, will reduce the potential feelings of panic and enable you to focus on your breathing which in turn will reduce your heart rate and, you've guessed it, reconnect your thinking brain. There is no suggestion that you undertake role play in order to practise but do take time to think through the process. Knowing what you need to say and do, how to arrange your face and what you need to do next will make a difficult situation much easier to manage.

You will also need to consider how much control and agency children and young people have once they have made a disclosure. In Chapter Seven, we talk about trauma informed practice and how children and young people can be supported to make choices and feel empowered in safeguarding. While you need to follow a particular process, as much as you can make sure that the child or young person who has experienced abuse or trauma is able to make decisions as to how things are managed (Wilson, Pence and Conradi, 2013).

Finally, make sure that you know what to do once the child or young person has disclosed to you so that you can explain to them what will happen next. This will be detailed in your school's safeguarding policy, which is why it is essential that you read it before you start at the school or as part of your induction (Chapter One). It should tell you who you tell, probably the Designated Safeguarding Lead (DSL), how you reach them if the disclosure is serious enough to warrant immediate action and where and how you need to record the information from the child or young person. (You can see all of this process in Figure 4.1 below)

```
┌─────────────────────────────────────────┐
│ Make sure you stop anything else that   │
│ you are doing – this signals to the     │
│ child or young person that you are      │
│ listening.                              │
└─────────────────────────────────────────┘
                    ↓
┌─────────────────────────────────────────┐
│ Give them space and time to tell you    │
│ what they need to say in their own      │
│ words – don't try and jump in and       │
│ interupt or interpret what is being     │
│ said.                                   │
└─────────────────────────────────────────┘
                    ↓
┌─────────────────────────────────────────┐
│ Make sure that you keep your face and   │
│ body language as open as possible       │
│ without expressing shock or disbelief   │
│ (this is likely to put the child or     │
│ young person off telling you any more). │
└─────────────────────────────────────────┘
                    ↓
┌─────────────────────────────────────────┐
│ Let them know that they have done the   │
│ right thing by telling you – perhaps    │
│ practise the actual words that you      │
│ will use.                               │
└─────────────────────────────────────────┘
                    ↓
┌─────────────────────────────────────────┐
│ Make sure that you tell them that you   │
│ believe what they are telling you and   │
│ are taking it really seriously – again  │
│ practise the actual words you will use. │
└─────────────────────────────────────────┘
                    ↓
┌─────────────────────────────────────────┐
│ Don't make promises you cannot keep.    │
└─────────────────────────────────────────┘
                    ↓
┌─────────────────────────────────────────┐
│ Explain what you are going to do next – │
│ children and young people need to know  │
│ what will happen and who you are going  │
│ to tell.                                │
└─────────────────────────────────────────┘
```

Figure 4.1 What You Need to Do When a Child or Young Person Discloses

Case Study 4.1

Background
There were already concerns about potential neglect of Matthew. He often arrived at school late with dirty clothes and saying that he was hungry. A member of the school pastoral team had a regular drop in with Matthew to make sure that he was OK and his class teacher had been asked to log any potential signs of neglect so that the school could build a picture for a possible referral.

What Happened?
One Monday morning Matthew arrived at school late. Although this was not unusual the fact that he was upset was. As soon as the other children in the class were settled and working on their first maths challenge the class teacher spoke quietly to Matthew to ask if he was OK. He told her that he was but as he wiped his eyes on his sleeve the class teacher noticed a mark on Matthew's arm. He asked Matthew to come with him and went out into the corridor so the other children could not hear and then asked Matthew how he had got the mark on his arm. Matthew told him that his Step-dad had grabbed him and that he had other bruises where his Step-dad had then hit him. Matthew's teacher told him that he needed to tell the school's DSL. Matthew asked if he could show his teacher the bruises and then asked what would happen next. His teacher asked him to wait until the DSL had arrived and said that the DSL would make sure that he was helped so that he didn't get hurt again. The class teacher sent one of the other children to ask the DSL to come to the classroom.

The DSL and the class teacher looked at Matthew's bruises together and then she made a referral to Children's Social Care. A Social Worker came to school with a police officer and determined that Matthew was at risk of harm. While they were at school they called Matthew's Mum and asked her to come to school. They explained that it was not safe for Matthew to be with his Step-dad. She agreed that she needed to keep Matthew safe and made arrangements to go and stay with her mother, Matthew's grandma while the issues were resolved.

Reflective Questions
- How did Matthew's teacher respond to the disclosure – what did he do and what didn't he do?
- What safeguarding issues can you identify in the case study?
- How might you apply this case study/learning to your work with children or young people?

What to Do If You Are Concerned About a Child or Young Person

Sometimes you will have a concern about a child or young person but they will not voluntarily come and talk to you about what is going on in their lives. We explore how behaviour can be a form of communication in Chapter Six – however there are some other indicators that a child or young person might be experiencing abuse or trauma that you will need to explore, even if you are busy teaching.

Bruises or other signs of injury – If a child or young person appears in your classroom with bruises or injury you must ask them what happened. While there are obviously some quite ordinary explanations for injuries there are others that signal that a child is being abused (see Chapter Two). In asking the child or young person how they were hurt you are inviting a disclosure that you will have to respond to as was seen in Case Study 4.1.

Dramatic change in behaviour – If you have been able to build good relationships with the children and young people in your class (see Chapter Three), then you will know if they are behaving completely differently from normal. Again it is important that you, carefully, ask questions that allow them to disclose, even if that is that they are tired or hungry. Open-ended questions are better in these instances – how are you feeling? You're different today, what's up? And so on.

Dramatic change in appearance – Again, you should know the children and young people in your class well enough to spot if one of them looks or smells very different from normal. This can be a positive thing if both have improved but if both have deteriorated – a quiet, non-confrontational conversation asking open-ended questions will allow children and young people to explain so that you can know if there is something that you need to refer on.

For all other concerns about children and young people in your class(es), using the guidance in Chapter Two, make sure that you make a note of them. You can then discuss these with the DSL to help you decide about next steps before you talk to the child, young person, parent or carer. As you become more confident you will learn that some of your concerns are your responsibility to respond to and some need to be managed by the DSL we looked at some of these in Chapter One.

Lack of Communication

One of the key issues about communication between teachers and children and young people that is often forgotten is the fact that children who have experienced abuse or trauma may not be able to articulate what they have experienced. For some children and young people this is because they have blocked out what has happened to them and therefore cannot access the memory verbally. For others it will be because the abuse or trauma they have experienced was experienced at a time when they had no words to attach to the description of the memory. Others will suffer from language delay as a result of the effect of slowed neurological development due to the abuse or trauma. There will also be some children or young people for whom living in deprivation has so reduced their exposure to language that they have not developed the ability to use the rich language that is necessary to describe their lives and experiences (Wolf, 2008). This is in addition to children and young people who have a special educational need linked to their ability to communicate. We need to remember that if we have concerns about a child or young person, they may not be able to help us discern what has happened. We need to be patient and work with them – exploring language and other ways of expression. The DSL or other members of the safeguarding team in your school may be more experienced in this and should be able to give you support if you think a child or young person is struggling to disclose because of communication difficulties.

Once You Have Received a Disclosure

It is important that once a child or young person has disclosed abuse to you that you ensure that they are safe. Do not presume that they are even if they are in school – particularly if they have disclosed something that comes under the category of child-on-child or contextual abuse. If they or other children or young people are at immediate risk you will have to make sure that other colleagues are informed *immediately*. This may be challenging if you are the only teacher in the classroom, nevertheless it is vital that you alert the DSL or in bigger schools the person who is 'on call' for safeguarding that day. If this means sending a child or young person with a message, make sure you impress upon the messenger that the DSLs presence is required urgently so that they know to prioritise coming to your classroom.

If the child or young person is not at immediate risk of harm they may still be feeling quite emotional having told you about their experience(s). Make sure that you give them space – physical if you can but at the very least emotional. This might look like giving permission to use the toilet or reducing your expectation for learning and possibly communicating the need for space to other colleagues if the child or young person is moving on to other classes. Make sure that you are circumspect about explaining what exactly has been said to you – it is not your role to disseminate that information to anyone other than the DSL.

Case Study 4.2

Background
In the Case Study 4.1 we saw that Matthew had made a disclosure of physical abuse by his Step-Dad.

What Happened?
After the disclosure Matthew was not able to concentrate on his maths and was quite tearful. At break time the class teacher asked if Matthew needed anything. Matthew asked if he could go and spend some time with the member of the pastoral team that usually checked in with him. The class teacher went with Matthew to see if that could happen.

Matthew's emotional needs were prioritised over his learning as he was unable to focus for the rest of the day while arrangements were made for him and his Mum to move to his Grandma's.

> **Reflective Questions**
> - How did Matthew's teacher respond to Matthew – what did he do and what didn't he do?
> - Have you identified any other safeguarding issues in the case study?
> - How might you apply this case study/learning to your work with children or young people?

The System and What Next After a Disclosure or a Safeguarding Concern

The first thing to note here is that you should not approach any abuser that a child or young person has identified in their disclosure to you. This is particularly important if the abuser is one of your colleagues. As you will have seen in Chapter Two there is a very clear process that needs to be followed in the case of an 'allegation' against a member of staff. This can be jeopardised and also put you at risk if you talk to them about what a child or young person has said. If the abuser is a parent, relative or member of the community that the child or young person lives in – you approaching them can also put the child, young person, you or the school at risk so make sure that you follow the procedure as laid out in the school's safeguarding policy.

Telling the DSL: The most important thing once a child or young person has disclosed abuse or trauma to you is to tell the DSL as soon as possible so that they can do something about it. This is so that any urgent issues can be referred on to children's social care before the end of the school day. Do not make the judgement about whether the disclosure is serious enough for this yourself. There may be other pieces of information which you don't know about (often called the 'jigsaw' of evidence) that contribute to a bigger picture. The DSL will be able to use all of what she or he knows to make sure that the child or young person is not facing a risk of experiencing further harm by going home without and intervention.

In most schools telling the DSL is the most important thing – as you will see in the next section you will have to record the disclosure and many of the electronic systems that schools use will email the DSL and let them know that there is a new record on the system. However, DSLs are often very busy people, particularly if they have a teaching responsibility, so may not access their emails regularly throughout the school day. You will need to make it your first priority to make sure that the DSL knows that you have had a child or young person disclose to you and what has been said so they can decide what to do next. Finding them, or ringing them, and telling them supersedes any teaching and learning responsibilities, getting yourself a coffee or eating your lunch!

If you have noticed something concerning you may also want to speak to the DSL. Here you may have to make a judgement about how urgent it is. For example, if you have noticed a bruise or injury this needs an urgent conversation. If you have noticed a drastic change in behaviour, then this again needs an urgent conversation.

If, however, a child or young person seems quiet or looks like they have been crying you probably need to do some investigation before you speak to the DSL or record your concerns.

Case Study 4.3

Background
Gemma was usually a bubbly and talkative member of the geography class. There were no previous safeguarding concerns.

What Happened?
Gemma arrived at the lesson a little late and looking a bit dishevelled. She went to the back of the classroom and sat away from her friends. She didn't talk at all during the lesson and completed her work with her head down on the desk. While the class was packing up to leave the geography teacher quietly asked Gemma what was wrong. Gemma burst into tears and said that something bad had happened on her way to the geography class. The geography teacher was in a hurry to get to the next lesson which was on the other side of the school. She asked Gemma if she wanted the teacher to do anything about what had happened and Gemma told her that she did not want anyone to know.

The geography teacher only remembered the incident when she got home that evening. First thing on the following day she went to find the DSL and told him what had happened. He was not very happy!

Gemma had been sexually assaulted by one of the older students. By the time the DSL was told the physical evidence that could have been collected had been washed away by Gemma who had had a shower when she got home and put her uniform in the washing machine.

Reflective Questions
- What did the teacher in this case study do wrong?
- What safeguarding issues can you identify in the case study?
- How might you apply this case study/learning to your work with children or young people?

Recording the disclosure: Most policies require you to record what has been said to you. This recording is often now on an online portal of some sort with Child Protection Online Management System (CPOMS) and My Concern being two of the most popular. If you are using one of these online portals the child or young person's details will already be on the system – make sure that you are entering the information you have onto the right child or young person's record. If the school you are working in is still using a paper-based system make sure that you record the child or young person's name accurately and that you include the date and approximate time of the disclosure and sign to confirm that it is an accurate record of what was said.

When you are making a record of a disclosure or concern you need to remember the following:

- What the record will be used for
  - A record of the disclosure or concern for the child or young person's record and to enable accurate onward referral if necessary.
  - Tracking safeguarding and child protection trends in the school.
  - Court reports – if the disclosure or concern is serious enough and the care of the child or young person is in question – your record may form part of the evidence in court.
- Any information that you record might also be shared with other agencies as this is a key part of the arrangements for agencies working together (DfE, 2023).
- That any record you make may be part of a request for information under data protection regulations meaning that parents, carers or older children and young people can ask to see what you have written about them – this means you need to take care about what you write and how you write it.
  - Make sure that you avoid narrative – be accurate and concise about what was said, do not include anything that you have inferred.
  - Make sure that you do not include your opinions or what you think might be happening – facts only.
  - Follow your school's guidance in terms of how you refer to members of staff and other children or young people.

You also need to make sure that you only share the information that you have recorded with the DSL and any other nominated safeguarding staff. This protects the child or young person and you.

Case Study 4.5

These are two examples taken from an online safeguarding record management platform. Read them and then reflect:

Example 1 – Just generally very grubby this week and without things like jumper/bag. Behaving badly this week and won't talk about why. So will update in the next week.

Example 2 – The pupil showed me some pictures she had printed out of cats 'smoking' cannabis on the school computer. I asked why she had chosen those pictures and she said 'because I find them funny' and they were shared with her by someone she knows on Discord. I am concerned that she is being contacted online by adults that she doesn't know.

(Continued)

> **Reflective Questions**
> - What do you think about these records?
> - How would you improve them?
> - What safeguarding issues can you identify?
> - How might you apply this case study/learning to your work with children or young people?

Other Important Elements of Communication

In *Keeping Children Safe in Education* (DfE, 2024), it states that all school staff should know how to make a referral into Children's Social Care. In practice the DSL or DDSL will do this. It is however important that you know what the process is. This is so that if you witness abuse outside school and cannot contact the DSL in a suitable timeframe you know how to contact what most Local Authorities call the Multi Agency Safeguarding Hub (MASH) team (see Chapter Two) or 'Out of hours team'. If this is not in the school's policy make sure that you ask the DSL for this information.

Difficult Conversations

In many schools the responsibility for communicating with parents when there is a concern or a disclosure rests with the class teacher. Make sure that you are clear what your responsibility is by discussing the disclosure or your concern with the DSL and asking explicitly what they would like you to do. You may need to have a conversation with other children and young people about issues that have happened in school under the child-on-child abuse or contextual safeguarding categories. There may also be situations where you think that a child or young person needs additional support or that the DSL has not acted in the way that you think they should have. All of these communications will provide some level of challenge and might well feel like difficult conversations.

The key to managing these is, in the first instance, to tackle them rather than dodge them. Clive Lewis (2011) describes how not having difficult conversations reduces effectiveness, this is particularly important when we are trying to keep children and young people safe. In his very readable short book Clive describes a process to help overcome the awkward and sometimes fearful feelings one might have when there is a difficult conversation to be had, whoever that might be with. The process is summarised here and made relevant to safeguarding conversations.

The first thing you need to be aware of is that if you put off having these difficult conversations the situation is likely to get worse. If you can have the conversation sooner, rather than later you might be able to head off problems at the pass. For example, if you are able to have a conversation with a parent about how tired their child is the first time it happens it might mean that they ensure that the child or young person gets the sleep they need from now on. If they don't you will at least have made a record of the fact that they have been spoken to and that perhaps they are neglecting their child's basic needs.

You might need to prepare yourself for these types of conversations. Just as was suggested when we talked about practising what and how you are going to say when a child or young person discloses you need to think through what you need to say in a difficult conversation. How are you going to phrase the difficult message you have to deliver? Have you got some specific evidence that you need to talk about? Do you need to get across particular points? Do you need to get the person you are communicating with to agree to something at the end? Thinking about these in advance will enable you to focus when you are in the moment.

Difficult conversations often require you to be brave. You should not put yourself at risk of harm, but if the message that you are trying to get across is a difficult one it is likely that the person you are talking to will get upset or angry. Again visualising this and what you will do when this happens helps. Convincing yourself that it is just a 'moment' in your life but might make a difference for a child or young person for the whole of their life might also help build up your courage.

If you do need to actually practise the conversation – make sure that you do this with the right person in school. This will usually be the DSL so that you are not disclosing privileged information to other colleagues. However, if you are wanting to challenge the DSL you will need to find a trusted colleague or one of your network (see Chapter Five) in order to rehearse what you need to say.

Finally – take time after a difficult conversation to recover your equilibrium. While you may not be able to do this immediately, it is really important that you ensure your well-being when you have been involved in both difficult conversations and disclosures from children or young people (see Chapter Five).

Just one final word about difficult conversations – they are almost always easier to have in person or, if necessary, over the phone. Putting things in writing particularly via electronic communication can present issues. Electronic communications can lead to misunderstandings as people can misconstrue what you are trying to say. They can also be used as evidence of what you have said and, unless they have been very carefully worded, this can sometimes be problematic. If you have to use electronic or written communication, they are best left to simply saying – 'Please can we arrange a time to have a conversation'.

If you are lucky enough to be in a school where they have a process for supervision (see Chapter Five) that you can access and you need to have a difficult conversation you can use the safe space that it provides to rehearse the conversation. You can also use it to reflect on what you want to achieve and why it is causing you anxiety. With a skilled supervisor you will be enabled to connect fully with why the conversation will better keep a child or young person safe and how to keep yourself emotionally safe while you are having it.

Case Study 4.6

Background
Ella had come to school in clothes that were dirty and smelt both stale and of cigarettes. Her class teacher, Susie, had already spoken to her Mum about making sure that Ella's clothes were being washed. Ella's Mum had been quite rude to Susie the last time she had spoken to her. This time, Ella was also dirty – her finger nails were black as was the back of her neck. Susie had talked to the DSL who was already booked to have a conversation with another parent at the end of the day so Susie had been asked to have a conversation with Ella's Mum. Susie made sure that she knew what message the DSL wanted to be conveyed.

What Happened?
At the end of the day Susie asked Ella's Mum if she could come into the classroom. Once Susie had made sure that all the other children had been collected she took a deep breath and explained that Ella's clothes were dirty and smelt stale and of cigarettes again. She also said that Ella's nails and neck were dirty.

Ella's Mum started shouting that she knew how to care for her child and that Susie should not be telling her what to do. Susie let Ella's Mum shout and then told her that she had lived on a farm as a child and was often dirty and that this had made her feel embarrassed at school. Susie used this as an opportunity to remind Ella's Mum how horrible it might feel for Ella and asked if there was anything else she or school could do to support her to clean both Ella and her clothes. Ella's Mum admitted that she had not been able to get the hot water boiler repaired which meant that she couldn't get the clothes clean and Ella was refusing to have a cold bath.

The DSL arranged for the school's family support worker to make a charity referral for a replacement boiler.

Reflective Questions
- How did Ella apply the process for difficult conversations from Clive Lewis' book (Lewis, 2011)?
- What safeguarding issues can you identify?
- How might you apply this case study/learning to your work with children or young people?

It is important to remember that many safeguarding conversations will feel difficult. Hearing that a child or young person has been abused, thinking that a colleague might be harming a child or young person or talking to a parent who is defensive is not easy. While you have to be brave and have these conversations when they are necessary there is no shame in admitting that they are hard and seeking support to help you manage your feelings.

Maintaining Professional Communication Especially in Relation to Digital and Social Media

In the last section, we briefly explored how it is better to have difficult conversations with regards to safeguarding in person not putting what you think in writing as this can be misconstrued. Given the importance of personal and professional reputation it is relevant here to think about electronic communication in more general terms. What you say in writing can be used against you so think carefully about what you say in emails, texts and other digital communication methods to colleagues, even if you consider them to be friends. If a child protection or safeguarding allegation is made against you it may be necessary to prove your integrity. If you have said something indiscreet on WhatsApp, for example, that you thought was between you and another member of staff they may have to reveal this in any subsequent investigation.

While the above is unlikely there are regularly issues around digital and social media communication with children or young people and their relatives. As a teacher part of your obligations, in accepting the role, is to uphold the integrity of the profession and the reputation of the school. There will be very clear guidelines as to contacting children and young people online. This is usually only on the school system and in relation to events related to school. If you are related to a child or young person in the school or if you have a legitimate connection with a child or young person outside of school, for example you are their sports coach at a wholly separate club, you need to make sure that your line manager and potentially the Head Teacher know what your relationship or connection is. This is in order to protect you and the child or young person from accusations of impropriety.

These connections are particularly dangerous if carried out over social media where they might be visible to other members of the school or local community – so unless you are overseeing your own child's social media by being their 'friend' the best advice is not to have children and young people as connections on your social media. You should ensure that your social media profiles are as private as they can be (i.e. friends only) and that any photographs of you that are in the public domain are ones you would be happy for children, young people or their parents to see. This goes for your friends sharing or tagging you in their social media too.

Case Study 4.7

Joseph Nicholson was employed as an English teacher at Crypt Grammar School in Gloucester. He was engaged by a parent to privately tutor her son. He was convicted in August 2023 after he started sending increasingly sexualised messages to the boy, culminating in a request for naked photos. The boy told his mother and she raised the alarm (BBC, 2023).

(Continued)

> **Reflective Questions**
> - What role did digital communication play in this case?
> - What do you think would have happened if Joseph had only been able to communicate via digital message with the child's parent?
> - What do you think could have been done to better protect the boy involved?
> - What safeguarding issues can you identify?
> - How might you apply this case study/learning to your work with children or young people?

Not communicating with children and young people via digital or social media seems straight forward, particularly given the case study. What is more difficult is communication with parents or carers and other adult relations. Again this is more complex if you are related to the child or young person or have a legitimate connection, i.e. like the aforementioned sports club. However, unless this is the case – the best way to protect yourself is to make sure that you do not engage in social media or digital communication with parents or carers adult relatives. If you have a legitimate reason, again make sure that the Head Teacher is aware of who you are in contact with in order to protect both your own and the school's reputation.

Even if you are not connected to children, young people, parents, or carers colleagues take care about what you publish on your publicly available posts. Many schools are now conducting online searches as part of their safer recruitment practices which are part of the safeguarding system. Schools are checking for comments that are dangerous, libellous or discriminatory – at the moment the systems that are used are only checking things that are in the public domain. If they can see them then so can anyone connected to your school. Don't say or do anything publicly that you would not want to defend if you are asked to do so by the Head Teacher. You may also want to think about what you publish in private on social media too. There may come a time when these posts are checked too and even if they are not – once you have posted something in your network you do not have control over where else it might be shared and who else might see it.

> ### Case Study 4.8
>
> #### Background
> Katie had started a job at a local secondary school. She was enjoying it and managing her workload well.
>
> #### What Happened?
> Katie went out with her best friend on her hen night. They went to the local town and were all dressed in short white dresses in stockings and suspenders. A number of her

friends took photos and uploaded them to Instagram including picture of Katie drinking cocktails out of a jug. One friend's Instagram account was not private and a number of parents saw the photographs as it was a small town and the hashtags brought the images up on both their feeds and those of their children. These parents complained to the school that this was not a good example to be setting to their children.

Katie was asked to meet with the Head Teacher who was disappointed that Katie had put herself and the school in the position that parents had complained. Katie received a written warning which would remain on her record for two years. She had to work hard to win back the respect of the children and young people in the school, her colleagues and the parent community.

Reflective Questions
- What role did digital communication play in this case?
- What could Katie have done to protect herself?
- What safeguarding issues can you identify?
- How might you apply this case study/learning to your work with children or young people?

Summary for This Chapter

In this chapter, we have looked at what you need to do if a child or young person discloses abuse or trauma to you. We have thought about the communication needed whether they have disclosed or whether you have a safeguarding concern. We have also explored some ideas that will help when you are required to have difficult conversations with regards to safeguarding issues. Finally, we have thought about digital and social media communications and how these are linked to your personal and professional integrity.

References

BBC (2023). Available at: https://www.bbc.co.uk/news/uk-england-gloucestershire-66658968 [Accessed 4.11.23].

Department for Education (DfE) (2023) *Working Together to Safeguard Children*. Available at: https://assets.publishing.service.gov.uk/media/65803fe31c0c2a000d18cf40/Working_together_to_safeguard_children_2023_-_statutory_guidance.pdf [Accessed on 17.2.24].

Department for Education (DfE) (2024) *Keeping Children Safe in Education*. London: DfE. Available at: https://www.gov.uk/government/publications/keeping-children-safe-in-education-2 [Accessed 24.5.24].

Lewis, C. (2011) *Difficult Conversations: 10 Steps to Becoming a Tackler Not a Dodger* Gloucester: Globis Mediation Group.

Wilson, C., Pence, D.M., Conradi, L. (2013) 'Trauma Informed Care' *Encyclopaedia of Social Work*. Available at: https://doi.org/10.1093/acrefore/9780199975839.013.1063 [Accessed 26.3.24].

Wolf, M. (2008) *Proust and the Squid* Cambridge: Icon Books.

5
Well-Being

> **Chapter Aims**
>
> - To explore teacher well-being strategies.
> - To explore pupil well-being.
> - To explore the physical and emotional aspects of well-being.
> - To explore how schools look after the well-being of both staff and pupils.

Introduction

Staff and pupil well-being are intrinsically linked, through both the physical and emotional connection. This chapter explores the link and sets out what needs to be in place to safeguard well-being across the school – including examples of how schools can address well-being. It also looks at how the individual classroom practitioner can recognise when they need support and where to go to get that support. It will also make clear the difference between well-being and safeguarding so that teachers are clear when and how to refer.

Teacher Well-Being

If you are feeling stressed how does this show up in your behaviour? In Chapter Six, we will look at behaviour as communication for children and young people. Here we are going to look at how your behaviour, that of your professional colleagues, your family and your friends also communicates how adults are feeling.

If you are stressed and grumpy at home, you may be able to admit that your behaviour is because you're not feeling great. Even if you aren't able to admit why you are behaving badly you are probably not very good company and those around you are likely to avoid interacting with you until you are in a better space. Unfortunately for the children and young people in your class(es) they don't have this option. They have to experience all your behaviour irrespective of whether you are your best self or one who is considerably under par. So, what do you need to do to recognise when your behaviour is communicating something negative to the children and young people you teach and what do you do about it once you recognise it?

Recognising How You Are Feeling and Behaving in Relation to Your Well-Being

> as we get older, we tend to forget how to listen to our bodies – *adults have the same central nervous system as they had when they were children* but over time learn to ignore them with a shift away from recognising our minds and bodies are connected. (Lea-Weston, 2022 n.p.)

For starters, how often do you neglect your physical needs when you are busy at school? Teachers regularly ignore these needs, often not hydrating or eating nutritious food. Many teachers will tell you that they often don't even have time to go to the toilet! None of these behaviours are healthy. They will have an impact on how present you can be in the classroom, whether you can carry out the essential relationship work discussed in Chapter Three and be in tune with the children or young people. The behaviours will also reduce the effectiveness of your immune system making you more susceptible to the inevitable germs in school, perhaps even leading to more serious ill-health.

In recent years, a huge amount of research has been carried out into how, as humans, we are interlinked. How our central nervous systems form a sort of network where our behaviours influence each other (Olson and Cozolino, 2014) – see Chapter Eight. One of the key reasons then to take proper care of ourselves is because it is only through doing this that we are able to properly care for the children and young people in our classes.

Many schools have well-being policies and strategies – these should start with ensuring that you have time to eat, drink and go to the toilet. If you are looking for your first teaching role in school, then make sure that the school that you choose to work in puts these basic physical needs first. They will expect that you will prioritise these for the children and young people that you work with as will be explored in later chapters.

Making sure that you eat nutritious food is down to you and while this doesn't mean that you shouldn't eat 'unhealthy' food it does mean that you should think about food – planning for when you are busy at school and make sure you are eating some food that boosts your energy and your physical systems. Alongside this, think about how you can make sure you are hydrated – especially when you are expected to be on duty during break times. You may think that neglecting these things won't have a huge impact on your daily performance as a teacher; however, if we take a leaf out of elite sport and the words of Dave Brailsford 'the aggregation of marginal gains' (Clear, n.p. n.d.) – the accumulation of lots of small acts helps us to achieve the best we can and this is an important way of making sure we look after our own well-being.

Once you have taken care of your basic physical needs you need to think about your emotional and psychological needs. How often do you check in with these and nourish them? This will look different for every individual. It might be that you need to be able to get outside to ensure that you are able to relax and recuperate. Or perhaps you need to swim or run to switch off your brain and revitalise your mind. You might be able to build your resources through cooking, painting or crafting, meeting friends, planning holidays, spending time with your family, curling up on the sofa with a good book or singing in a choir. Whatever it is that you need to keep you balanced, you need to make sure that you know what it is and build in time to do it. School well-being strategies or policies should recognise that people need different things for this. Creating team building or well-being events do not necessarily mean well-being to everyone. Again, make sure that the school you choose to work in when you apply for teaching roles provides what you need in terms of your well-being. There is an old adage 'you can't pour from an empty cup' and this is particularly true for teachers and your role as a 'frontline' safeguarding professional.

Mindfulness and Calming Rituals

We all have things that we do to help us keep calm. It is important that we know what these are and harness them both during the school day and outside of school. Whether these are breathing exercises, counting to ten, closing your eyes for a second or having something to fiddle with these techniques will help you to regulate yourself. This is a key skill both for your own well-being and that of the children and young people that you work with, particularly for those who are dysregulated as a result of trauma or abuse. We will explore this more in Chapters Six and Seven. Making sure that you know how you recognise when you are dysregulated and that you know how to regulate and re-engage your central nervous system is a vital tool in your teaching toolbox.

Mindfulness is a particular method of calming or regulating. Mind, the mental health charity, describes mindfulness as 'a technique you can learn which involves noticing what's happening in the present moment, without judgement' (Mind, n.d. n.p.). It has become a very popular way of managing stress, looking after well-being and enabling the processing of thoughts. There are also a number of apps and YouTube videos that you can use to help you master the techniques. If you have not already explored mindfulness it is worth giving it some time to see if it is useful for you in managing your own well-being. If you find it is not for you, make sure you that you know what does help you and build that into your daily and weekly activities.

Strategies for Supporting Your Own Well-Being

In the previous section, a long list of what might help you nourish your emotional resilience was provided alongside thinking about calming rituals and mindfulness. There may, however, be times when these past times or relaxation activities are not enough to sustain you. This is particularly likely if you have been the recipient of a particularly distressing disclosure from a child or young person (the practicalities of this are covered in Chapter Four), you have a child or young person in your class who has extreme trauma responses (Chapters Six and Seven) on a regular basis, you have had a number of upsetting incidents happen in a short period of time or you experience a personal crises.

Finding it difficult to manage your well-being in the face of difficulty does not make you weak or a bad teacher. You need to feel comfortable with acknowledging that you need something more and seek out support. This might look like talking with a trusted colleague, accessing supervision (described later in this chapter), leaning on your professional network, counselling or accessing free support through https://www.educationsupport.org.uk/. Whatever it is that helps you when things seem overwhelming, make sure that you take time to get back the balance needed to face a class of children or young people. If you need to take time off work make sure that you visit your general practitioner (GP) who can provide you with the certification you need to provide for sickness absence. Your school should also have access to occupational health support or a well-being helpline, these can be accessed while you are taking the time you need and once you feel ready to return to work. If your school is not supportive around your well-being, particularly if you have had to take time off then please seek the support of your union or if you are a student teacher the university well-being team.

Case Study 5.1

Background
Ethan was a student teacher who enjoyed playing his guitar in a band. He was working in a busy comprehensive school where his mentor regularly checked in on his well-being.

What Happened
As Ethan's teaching practice progressed he found it hard to keep up with all the planning, marking and other paperwork. He didn't see anyone else struggling so in an attempt to keep on top of everything he gave up the band, becoming reclusive and not really seeing any of his friends.

A couple of weeks before the end of his teaching practice his mentor asked if he was all right as it had been noticed that he was spending most of his time in a classroom and had become very quiet.

Ethan explained how he had been struggling with the workload and that he had given up playing in the band and his social interactions to keep on top of it. His mentor helped Ethan work on a plan to manage the work and encouraged him to re-engage with his social activities, explaining that his mood had been affected by giving them up and the young people that he taught had started to notice.

Reflective Questions
- What do you think Ethan should have done to protect his own well-being?
- How did Ethan's school support his well-being?
- What effect do you think Ethan's deteriorating well-being was having on the young people he was teaching?
- How do you think the information in this case study links to safeguarding?
- How might you apply this case study/learning to your work with children or young people?

School Well-Being Strategies and Policies

Once you have thought about how you need to prioritise your well-being you need to make sure it is recognised by the school you choose to teach in. As has already been mentioned many schools have published strategies or policies – if you are applying for a job make sure you look on their website or ask for it along with the recruitment pack. The best of these make it clear that teaching can be stressful and that they recognise the hard work of the staff in the school to support the well-being, safeguarding and learning of the children and young people. A school that values its staff first and foremost will have staff well-being at its heart so that staff can do what they are there to do, irrespective of whether there are regular staff socials or events for well-being.

Case Study 5.2

Background

Diane worked in a busy inner city primary school. The children that she taught faced many challenges in their lives and this meant that they often struggled to manage themselves in the classroom and apply themselves to their learning. Diane, like most teachers, was hardworking and diligent, often finding herself working late and at weekends. As a result, she had stopped running at the weekends and was existing primarily on ready meals and chocolate.

Diane's school had a well-being policy which detailed the care that the staff were entitled to including one staff meeting per half term being dedicated to staff well-being.

What Happened?

Towards the end of Diane's first half term which was eight weeks long Diane received an all-staff email detailing that the staff well-being staff meeting was to be a social event in a local busy pub. The thought of this was completely overwhelming for Diane who was exhausted. Instead of going to the social event she just went home and went to bed feeling as though she was letting herself and everyone else down.

The following day her mentor came to find her. Diane broke down and told her how she felt.

Diane and her mentor discussed what well-being looked like for Diane. This was then fed back to the senior leadership team who reviewed the policy and thought about how to better support the well-being of all staff including those who were new to the school and the profession.

Reflective Questions
- What do you think Diane could have done to protect her own well-being?
- What effect do you think Diane's deteriorating well-being was having on the young people she was teaching?
- How do you think the information in this case study links to safeguarding?
- How might you apply this case study/learning to your work with children or young people?

Supervision

Some schools have begun to provide supervision. This type of well-being support comes from medicine (clinical supervision) and social work (often reflective supervision). In schools, the word supervision has historically only been used in relation to making sure there are enough adults to look after the children or young people. However, there is growing understanding that supervision for education professionals is a tool that can support the emotional well-being of teachers and therefore promote the well-being of children and young people.

> At its simplest, supervision is a 'professional conversation' [...]. Supervision is therefore a method of support for staff so that they can provide for the needs of the students and to build safe cultures for everyone in the school community. (Sturt and Rowe, 2018 p7)

One of the key things about supervision that is different from the support that you will have from a mentor or colleague is that is designed to help you re-connect with yourself. Managing your own regulation, supporting the well-being of your central nervous system while thinking about the well-being of the children and young people that you work with. This process is iterative and supports your capacity for creativity, compassion, humour, kindness, connection and relationships.

Schools that have implemented this for all staff are few and far between however some schools have begun to offer it to their senior leaders and Designated Safeguarding Leads (DSLs) in recognition of how safeguarding can take an emotional toll. In the second edition of their book *Using Supervision in Schools* (2023), Sturt and Rowe explain that

> supervision offers a space to explore the emotional labour of caring for and about children. (Sturt and Rowe, 2023 p11)

If you are fortunate enough to work in one of the schools that are implementing this sort of support and feel that your emotional well-being is suffering particularly as a result of the safeguarding issues experienced by the children or young people in your class or classes, then do ask if you can access supervision. There is growing evidence that supervision in education has a positive impact on both teachers and children and young people (Edwards, 2023).

Case Study 5.3

Background

The multi-academy trust that Fatima worked in had recently begun to implement supervision for those working in the safeguarding team. The trust safeguarding lead had been trained to carry out supervision with her supervision being provided by an external supervisor. A policy had been agreed across the trust and the DSLs in each school had started receiving regular supervision.

Fatima taught in a class with a number of children who were on child protection and child in need (CIN) plans. This was not unusual for her school but as an Early Career Teacher (ECT) Fatima was still learning to manage all the needs of the children in her class.

What Happened?

One of the children in her class came to tell her that her friend, Sara, had some bruises on her leg. When Fatima checked Sara had shown her bruises on the inside of her thigh. Fatima realised that this was very serious and sent a message with a sensible child for the DSL to come at once. The DSL made sure that an immediate referral to social care was made for Sara. Social workers and the police came to speak to Sara and she was taken into emergency foster care. She continued to come to school once this had happened and the DSL asked for Fatima to carry on as normal being kind to Sara.

Fatima was glad that she had acted quickly to protect Sara, Sara was now safe and she could continue their professional relationship. However, Fatima found it difficult that no further information had been shared with her and found herself obsessing about what had happened to Sara. After a while she decided to go and talk to the DSL.

The DSL explained that often those who take the first disclosure do not find out any more detail and offered Fatima a one-off supervision session to help her manage her feelings about the situation. During the session the DSL helped Fatima to think about why she was having obsessive thoughts about what had happened to Sara, whether this was affecting their ongoing relationship, how to manage these feelings and how Fatima might approach similar situations in the future.

Reflective Questions

- Why do you think Fatima was not told anything further about Sara's situation?
- How did Fatima take care of her own well-being and what did the school do to support?
- What safeguarding issue does this case study highlight?
- How might you apply this case study/learning to your work with children or young people?

There are times when the well-being of teachers and the well-being of children or young people are 'potentially in conflict' (Roffey, 2012 p14). Do make sure that you understand the balance that is needed and if you find that your well-being is beginning to suffer as the result of a child or young person's challenges speak to your senior colleagues or professional support network.

Professional Network

This has been mentioned a number of times in the chapter – this will be a group of people that you can trust and talk to in confidence when you need to. As you grow into the profession you will find people who can fulfil this role. Make sure that you choose wisely so that these people do not cause you embarrassment by disclosing your worries and concerns publicly.

Well-Being of Children and Young People

There are many definitions of well-being and with the rise in concerns around mental health these have often become conflated. Martin Seligman's definition of well-being seems reasonable as he suggests that well-being

> Consists of having *positive emotions*, being *engaged* in an activity, having good *relationships* with other people, finding *meaning* in one's life and a sense of *accomplishment* in the pursuit of ones' goals. (Seligman, 2011 quoted from Burr, 2022 p2)

From this we can see the relevance of well-being to being a classroom practitioner. You should be concerned with all the aspects in italics as part of what you do for all the children and young people that you teach. Well-being is also clearly linked to safeguarding. If we return to the definition of safeguarding taken from *Working Together to Safeguard Children* (DfE, 2023) we can see that aspects are clearly related to well-being not child protection. It is this that makes safeguarding a more holistic approach to ensuring that children and young people get the best possible start in life:

- providing help and support to meet the needs of children as soon as problems emerge;
- ensuring that children grow up in circumstances consistent with the provision of safe and effective care; and
- taking action to enable all children to have the best outcomes.

(DfE, 2023 pp7, 8)

So, let's have a look at what you can do to support well-being in the classroom and therefore ensure that you are providing the holistic support for safeguarding that is your responsibility both under the latest *Keeping Children Safe in Education* (DfE, 2024a) and *Initial Teacher Training (ITT) and Early Career Framework (ECF)* (DfE, 2024b).

Supporting the development of positive emotions enables children and young people to engage in learning (or activity in Seligman's definition). You can do this by smiling and showing the children and young people that you work with that you like them, in the first instance, building the relationships that we explored in Chapter Three. Positive emotions are also developed by having those around you being positive – hence the importance of looking after your own well-being. Creating a classroom culture where children are encouraged to feel valued through the environment (Chapter Eight) and through the behaviours of the adults and other children and young people will also contribute to this positive feeling. Establishing calming rituals (such as mindfulness or routines) in the classroom will also help the well-being of children and young people (Olson and Cozolino, 2014).

The learning activity is also a vital part of well-being – make sure that you are meeting children and young people's learning needs and engaging them in a way that means that they are intellectually stimulated without being pushed too hard or too fast. This is particularly important for children and young people with diagnosed or suspected neurodiversity. You will know when the vast majority of the children are too far 'out of their depth' with the learning from the emotional temperature in the room and this will affect everyone's well-being including your own. To ensure that this doesn't happen make sure that you are confident that you know what children and young people need to be working towards, how to set them goals or targets and how to break this down into steps so that they can feel accomplished at each stage in their development. This book is not about learning pedagogy, Forster and Eperjesi (2019) is a good source for primary teachers and Hoath and Podesta (2023) for secondary teachers; however, good teaching is a vital source of well-being in your classroom.

> ### Case Study 5.4
>
> #### Background
> Year 9 in the special school that Stephanie taught in had a number of young people with diagnoses of neurodiversity and difficult safeguarding backgrounds. They were often 'fidgety' and unable to focus on their work particularly after lunchtime.
>
> #### What Happened?
> One particularly challenging afternoon, on a whim, Stephanie decided to take the young people into the school grounds and carry out their reading activities outside. Some of the young people were much more able to focus on their reading outside. A couple of the young people found an unusual looking plant and wanted to use the iPad to find out what it was which resulted in them spending some time reading information on the internet. The others spent time exploring the forest school area which was not being used by anyone else that afternoon, teaching themselves how to make a bridge over a muddy patch.
>
> #### Reflective Questions
> - How did Stephanie take care of both the well-being of the young people in her class and her own?
> - What strategies do you think were in place in the school that Stephanie taught that enabled her to care for everyone's well-being?
>
> *(Continued)*

- How do you think this links to safeguarding?
- How might you apply this case study/learning to your work with children or young people?

What Is the Difference Between Well-Being and Safeguarding?

It is really important to be clear about what you should be supporting as part of your role as a caring and compassionate professional teacher, what you should be recording when you do this and what needs more immediate action in terms of safeguarding?

First of all, any issues that fall into the categories defined in Chapter Two should be immediately referred to the DSL. While they may lead to well-being issues that you can support in the classroom child protection should never just be managed by a single person and certainly not a lone class teacher. Any issues that may cross the boundary into mental health issues such as self-harm, eating disorders, anxiety or depression should be referred to the right person in your school – this will likely be the nominated mental health lead. In reality this is often the DSL and even if it isn't they should probably know about any obvious mental health issue. If you think that a child or young person has experienced a loss or bereavement, then you should also make sure that the DSL or mental health lead knows.

These are fairly straightforward – it becomes more complex with some more grey areas. For example, what do you do about a child or young person who is tired or one who is hungry or one who finds it hard to even try the learning. In the first two examples they need to be recorded on the school's online management system as a concern or whatever categories the school uses. This will enable further incidents to be tracked leading to a judgement by the DSL as to whether it is something more serious than a one-off or occasional tiredness or hunger. It is also your responsibility to follow this up in the first instance. If you are new to the class, make sure that you check there have not been any previous concerns. As long as this is the first instance, unless your school specifically determines otherwise, ring the child or young person's parent so that they know that their child was tired or hungry.

In the example of a child or young person who finds it hard to try the learning or in a further example of a child or young person not being able to focus on their work without adult support you will need to explore some issues as the class teacher before you log a concern. Both these issues could just be a child or young person who is under confident. It could also be that the learning is not targeted at their needs or they have an unrecognised learning need. It could also be an indication of other issues (see Chapter Six). Do not jump to conclusions! Adjust the learning and the support the child or young person is receiving – ask them what it is that is causing them difficulty. Talk to other colleagues to gauge whether the behaviour is specific to your classroom. If, after you have supported and other colleagues confirm that the child or young person experiences difficulties elsewhere, have a conversation with the Special Education Needs Coordinator (SENCO) and decide together whether this is a safeguarding or a learning issue.

In all instances where you might be thinking that a child has well-being issues, beyond the ordinary occasional feeling a bit 'off', if you are not sure if the issue needs to be referred or not it is always safer to have a conversation with the DSL. Better to be told that there is no need to record or refer than find out that something that you have known about for a while is part of a big picture that needed immediate action.

Case Study 5.5

Background
Niamh was generally hard working, although she struggled with the content of the lessons and had support for her literacy skills. She had friends in the school and was often keen to help others and class teachers.

What Happened
Niamh fell asleep in the back of Eric's maths class. At the end of the lesson Eric asked Niamh if she was all right. She said that she had just had a late night and that she was sorry and that it wouldn't happen again.

Eric was not sure about what to do so he mentioned it to his ECT mentor who also taught Niamh. She confirmed that Niamh had fallen asleep in her class the previous day too so they went to speak to the DSL. As Eric had a good relationship with Niamh he was asked to have another conversation with Niamh, gently telling her that he knew that she had fallen asleep in other classes too.

When Eric spoke to Niamh she admitted that she was sleeping on the sofa with her younger brother at her Mum's friend's house as they had been evicted from their home.

Eric passed this information to the DSL who spoke to Mum and with her consent made a referral to Children's Social Care to get the family some support to find housing.

Reflective Questions
- How did Eric discover that there was a more serious issue than just Niamh's well-being to manage?
- What was the safeguarding issue and how was Eric involved in managing it?
- How might you apply this case study/learning to your work with children or young people?

The Link Between Teacher and Children or Young People's Well-Being

Sue Roffey's (2012) study explored the link between pupil well-being and teacher well-being. She identifies a number of themes that bear consideration here to support you in your classroom and in making sure that the school you chose to work in has your well-being and that of the children and young people at the centre of all that they do. In some places the themes of Roffey's original have been collapsed together to make sense of practicalities for you to implement to support both your own well-being and that of the children and young people in your class.

Values – 'relational values of respect, acceptance and care [have] to extend both from and to all staff' (Roffey, 2012 p11) and these need not to be left to chance. These are discussed further in Chapter Three in terms of building them with children and young people. It is important to remember that these need to be modelled by senior leaders to all staff and between colleagues too – this sends clear messages to everyone in the school that how you feel matters.

Belonging – feeling that you are a part of something appeared to be key for both health and learning. For both children and young people and adults this feeling enables a 'greater willingness to abide by the norms and values' (Roffey, 2012 p11) of the school. This feeling of belonging should also include what we now refer to as inclusion – where all members of the school community feel accepted for whom they are and therefore feel comfortable in the environment.

Creating a safe environment – we will discuss this in more detail in Chapter Eight.

Ensuring Behaviour is well supported – we will discuss this in more detail in Chapter Six.

Positive feelings and resilience – this is not only about the values as described above but also about how school support strengths based approaches where children, young people and adults have their talents and abilities recognised irrespective of how well these are performed. Roffey's study also identifies here the 'power of fun and laughter to support wellbeing and learning' (Roffey, 2012 p14).

> **Reflective Question**
>
> Think about these themes – how have teachers that you know or have observed performed the behaviours or created the environments where they thrive?

Summary for This Chapter

In this chapter, we have explored your well-being. We have looked at strategies for you to care for yourself and what schools should be doing to support teacher well-being, including supervision. We then explored children and young people's well-being and what responsibilities you have for this and what you can do to support it. The difference between well-being and more urgent safeguarding issues have then been made clear. Finally, we have explored how your well-being and that of children and young people are interlinked and what you might need to think about in the classroom to support you both.

References

Burr, R. (2022) *Self-Worth in Children and Young People*. St Albans: Critical Publishing.

Clear, J. (n.d.) *This Coach Improved Every Tiny Thing by 1 Percent and Here's What Happened*. Available at: https://jamesclear.com/marginal-gains [Accessed 26.3.24].

Department for Education (DfE) (2023) *Working Together to Safeguard Children*. London: DfE. Available at: https://www.gov.uk/government/publications/working-together-to-safeguard-children–2 [Accessed 26.3.24].

Department for Education (DfE) (2024a) *Keeping Children Safe in Education*. London: DfE. Available at: https://www.gov.uk/government/publications/keeping-children-safe-in-education–2 [Accessed 26.5.24].

Department for Education (DfE) (2024b) *Initial Teacher Training and Early Career Framework*. Available at: https://www.gov.uk/government/publications/initial-teacher-training-and-early-career-framework [Accessed 16.2.24].

Edwards, H. (2023) *Reflective Supervision in Education*. London: Jessica Kingsley Publishers.

Forster, C. and Eperjesi, R. (eds) (2019) *Teaching the Primary Curriculum*. London: SAGE.

Hoath, L. and Podesta, E. (2023) *Professional Studies for Secondary Teaching*. London: Learning Matters.

Lea Weston, L. (2022) *Teacher Wellbeing Is the Beginning of Pupil Wellbeing*. Available at: https://dreamachine.world/2022/09/21/teacher-well-being-blog/ [Accessed 7.10.23].

Mind (n.d.) Available at: https://www.mind.org.uk/information-support/drugs-and-treatments/mindfulness/about-mindfulness/ [Accessed 16.2.24].

Olson, K. and Cozolino, L. (2014) *The Invisible Classroom*. New York: W. W. Norton & Company.

Roffey, S. (2012) 'Pupil wellbeing- Teacher wellbeing: Two sides of the same coin?' *Education and Child Psychology*, 29(4), pp. 8, 17.

Seligman, M. (2011) *Flurish: A New Understanding of Happiness and Wellbeing: The Practical Guide to Using Positive Psychology to Make You Happier and Healthier*. Philadelphia, PA: Nicolas Brearley Publishing.

Sturt, P. and Rowe, J. (2018) *Using Supervision in Schools*. Shoreham-by-Sea: Pavilion.

Sturt, P. and Rowe, J. (2023) *Using Supervision in Schools*, 2nd edition. Shoreham-by-Sea: Pavilion.

6

Behaviour as Communication

Chapter Aims

- To explore how child or young person's behaviour might communicate what is happening to them.
- To develop strategies to support child or young person's communicating behaviours.
- To develop strategies to enable child or young person to communicate differently.

Introduction

Everything we do says something about what we are thinking and feeling. This chapter sets out how an understanding of this leads to a safeguarding approach rather than a traditional behaviour management approach. It builds on Chapter Three and the relationships that are vital for understanding what child or young person is saying through their behaviour. This understanding is set out as a means for discovering abuse over and above traditional disclosure.

How Do We Communicate Through Behaviour?

Have you ever felt upset about something but had to be somewhere where it is not appropriate to share how you feel? Then, despite your best efforts someone asks if you are OK because they have noticed that you are a bit off. Or perhaps something has made you really angry but you are somewhere you can't express it – so you suppress it, only for you to take it out on a loved one when you get home. These are examples of how you are communicating through your behaviour. In the first instance, the person who asks if you are OK has picked up on something you are doing that has communicated to them that everything is not well with you. In the second example, your loved one is being told in no uncertain terms that something earlier on made you angry and you are frustrated that you had to suppress it. Now, imagine that you are a child or young person and everything at home is frightening – your parents are always arguing and your dad is often violent towards you and your siblings as well as your mum. When you get to school it is generally calm so you feel safe. Then a child or young person in your class starts shouting, you feel frightened and you respond by tipping over a desk and hiding behind it. From the outside this might look like 'poor or challenging behaviour'. In many schools, behaviours such as these receive a sanction with the child or young person being removed from the classroom before receiving a detention – or if it is a frequent occurrence a suspension or exclusion. However, with the benefit of the information about the home life of this child or young person we can see the subsequent behaviour as a communication of fear and distress as a result of exposure to domestic abuse. Given this simple example think about how child or young person might respond to the multitude of safeguarding issues that we explored in Chapter Two communicating them through behaviour. As Dr Ross Greene suggests, children or young people with a trauma history do not need any further punishment (Greene, 2014).

It is worth introducing the concept of trauma here. In short trauma is how we carry negative experiences with us. For children and young people these experiences are sometimes referred to as Adverse Childhood Experiences – ACEs (Felitti et al., 1998). The generally more ubiquitous term 'trauma' is used in this book as it covers a wider range of experiences, all of which can have a significant impact on our behaviour. This will be covered in more detail in Chapter Seven.

While it is impossible to describe here the cause of every sort of behaviour that you might see – it is possible to summarise the sorts of behaviour a child or young person might demonstrate which are likely to be communicating that they have an unmet need which may be as a result of a safeguarding issue or trauma. As you saw in Chapter Four, it is important to be alert to the fact that children and young people are often unable to articulate their experiences and often communicate through their behaviour or actions.

Types of Behaviour That Might Indicate Distress

When a child or young person has experienced a distressing event they may process it as traumatic which can then stimulate their survival instinct, particularly when 'triggered' – see Chapter Seven. This can then result in the following behaviours.

Fight – a child or young person may become angry or aggressive, physically or verbally attacking others in the vicinity. They may also respond by harming themselves.

Flight – a child or young person may retreat from a situation physically or mentally. This might result in them running away, hiding or retreating emotionally. It is a high energy behaviour displaying anxiety or panic.

Freeze – a child or young person may stop all activity including 'playing dead'. They may be rendered unable to communicate or dissociate themselves from the situation.

Fawn – a child or young person may become overly compliant and mask their feelings and their normal behaviours, trying to appease those around them.

Flop – a child or young person may faint or become completely floppy. They may also respond by becoming sick or ill.

> ### Case Study 6.1
>
> ### Background
> Kyle arrived at school in a hoodie – with the hood up and wouldn't remove it. He slumped into his seat and would not engage with anyone. He wouldn't answer when his name was called and did no work.
>
> ### What Happened?
> One of the others in the class pulled down his hood. Kyle 'flipped his lid'. He pushed his chair back and over as he stood up, swiped everything onto the floor, pushed the teaching assistant out of the way and ran from the classroom.
>
> The Head Teacher was called as Kyle had then 'absconded' from school.
>
> ### Reflective Question
> - What do you think has happened here?
> - What safeguarding issues can you identify?
> - How might you apply this case study/learning with the children and young people that you work with?

If a child or young person in your class demonstrates any of these behaviours it is always worth exploring whether they are as a result of an unmet safeguarding need. While there is a need to follow the behaviour or relationship policy in your school, there is much you can do to support the child or young person or young person to regulate and then communicate verbally once they are calm. If you have been able to put the time and effort into building a relationship – as we explored in Chapter Three – this will enable you to read the behaviour that has happened or has been happening. Then using the communication skills from Chapter Four you will be able to elicit the information needed to identify and support the child or young person's needs being met. You will then be able to help promote changes in behaviour that will likely lead to better learning than the traditional behaviour sanction model.

Supporting Children and Young People Whose Behaviour Has Been Hijacked

The behaviours we have explored in the first part of this chapter can be a response to the impact of abuse on a child or young person's developing nervous system leading to an inability to emotionally self-regulate in any other way than through primitive behaviours. They can also be a response to the brain being absorbed in managing the emotions and crises that abuse creates, leaving no processing space for social and intellectual interaction at school – the child or young person is overwhelmed by their safeguarding needs and becomes dysregulated. These types of behaviours may also be as a result of neurodiversity, disability or other unmet needs – so it is important to work out what the behaviour is communicating.

> ## Case Study 6.2
>
> Let's return to Kyle from Case Study 6.1
>
> ### Background
> Kyle lived in a volatile household. His mother's partner could sometimes be kind, playful and full of fun. At other times he could be angry and violent. The extremes of behaviour meant that Kyle and his mother tiptoed around him at home, hoping that they didn't 'set him off'.
>
> On the morning of the incident described – there had been an angry row at home. Kyle's mother had been held by the throat just as Kyle was about to get some breakfast. He fled from the house so as not to see the outcome or aftermath.
>
> ### What Happened?
> By the time he got to school he was scared that his mother had been hurt, he was angry with himself for running and not staying to protect her and was anxious about what he might find when he got home. The lack of breakfast or a drink meant that he was also hungry and thirsty. All of this meant that he was not able to think straight – he was still in the kitchen re-living what he had lived through that morning. The pulling down of his hood was enough to galvanise his fight and flight behaviours. He instinctively ran for home – to protect his mother or perhaps quell the rising fear and anxiety about what he might find by getting home now rather than later.
>
> ### Reflective Questions
> - Now you know more detail about Kyle – what do you think the teacher could have done here to support Kyle and ensure a more successful transition into learning?
> - What safeguarding issues can you identify?
> - How might you apply this case study/learning with the children and young people that you work with?

While behaviours are often experienced as and called 'challenging' in the classroom they are even more difficult for the child or young person involved (Greene, 2014). In order to respond with a safeguarding approach, it is important to think about how and why they have been emotionally 'hijacked' and how you can then provide 'Connection before Correction', a phrase popularised by the psychiatrist Daniel Siegel (Siegel and Bryson, 2015). This not only links to the relationship work you will have carried out as a result of reading Chapter Three but is also key in the moment and immediate aftermath of the behaviour. The following process, for you to think about applying when faced with a child or young person in survival or dysregulated mode, is adapted from the work of Kim Golding (2015):

Notice – make sure that you are aware of what the children or young people in your classroom are doing. It is important that if warning signs are there that you notice them and use the information to decide what to do next – for example a child or young person who usually gives eye contact when they come into the classroom avoiding looking at you? Or perhaps a child or young person is red in the face or a child or young person who is normally talkative is particularly quiet. Knowing your children or young people well and what their 'normal' is, is key here.

Think – what you might need to do next, what does what you have noticed mean and how you might have to adjust in order to 'head off an incident at the pass'.

Pause – before you do anything. How are you feeling? If you are anxious or stressed about what you think is about to happen or what is happening, you will not be able to support a child or young person to regulate. What do you need to do to ensure that you are regulated first? In Chapter Five we explored what you do to make sure you are in the best possible position to support child or young person with safeguarding needs, how you connect with your own central nervous system. While you may not be able to take a break or step back from the moment if the child or young person's behaviour has already escalated pausing momentarily will help you to reconnect with your own regulation skills preventing you from getting defensive and perhaps combative with the child or young person you need to engage with.

Regulate – This is the key part of a safeguarding approach when a child or young person is communicating their needs or experiences through behaviour. If a child or young person is in full on fight, flight, freeze or flop (faun is slightly different) then they will not be able to engage in any cognitive process to calm down – no amount of asking them to make good choices will reach the thinking part of their brain, the prefrontal cortex. You will have to co-regulate with them in order to return them to a regulated state. This can only be done if you are regulated. It means talking calmly – no one ever calmed down with someone shouting at them! It can mean keeping up a steady but calm monologue for the child or young person to eventually tune into or it can mean being quiet. Giving space can also help – this is often difficult in a classroom, particularly if other children or young people are staring or getting involved. We will look at this some more in Chapter Eight where we will look at creating a safe environment. As much as possible move other children or young people away so that you can co-regulate with the child or young person in a space which is not crowded by others. Concentrate on keeping your heart rate and breathing calm – this helps the dysregulated child or young person to return their own heart rate and breathing to normal. This can be incredibly difficult especially if you are being physically or verbally abused by the child or young person in question. Visualisation techniques can be very useful in helping you to keep calm when there is chaos going on around you. Use the case study below to help you think about what you will do when you are faced with an extremely dysregulated child or young person.

Regulation might take some time – an example that is often used is that of a boiled kettle which takes over an hour to be completely cold again. A child or young person who has 'boiled over' may not be able to return to learning in the lesson but if you are able to complete the process they are more likely to return effectively to learning in the future.

If the situation is at any time unsafe for you or the other children or young people in the class, then you *must* follow the established protocols in the school to make sure that you do not subject any of you to the risk of harm from the dysregulated child or young person. However, if you have a good relationship with the child or young person it is important that you are involved in the next steps even if others have intervened to ensure the safety of everyone involved.

Case Study 6.3

Background

Philip was hot and bothered. He was offered a drink and refused. It was suggested that he take off his jumper – he refused to do this too. One of the other children in the class laughed (as it happens not at Philip). The teacher was standing next to Philip when he stood up and started yelling at the other child. She started talking to Philip in a very calm quiet voice, asking if he would like to leave the classroom with her. She carefully moved Philip's chair back and gave him space to move away from the desk. Philip's desk was the closest to the classroom door. By positioning herself between Philip and the rest of the class and calmly and quietly encouraging him to walk out through the open door she was able to remove Philip from the classroom with as little drama as possible.

What Happened?

The corridor was quieter and cooler than the classroom. The teacher encouraged Philip to look at her and then breathed with him to regulate his breathing. He soon looked less agitated and before long agreed to a drink of water. He returned to the classroom and sat quietly at his desk for the rest of the lesson – he was not able to engage in learning, but he was not disrupting the other children from their learning.

Reflective Questions
- What safeguarding issues can you identify?
- How might you apply this case study/learning with the children and young people that you work with?

Case Study 6.3 might seem like the perfect approach, so let's unpick how there was such a successful outcome in this situation using the model so far.

Notice – The teacher in this instance was well aware of Philip's difficult home life and the fact that he was being emotionally abused (bullied) by his older brother. She had also experienced situations before when Philip had really 'flipped his lid'. She recognised the signs: being hot, refusing to comply with requests to remedy feeling hot and so on.

Think – the previous incidents had promoted her thinking through how best to manage situations when Philip appeared overwhelmed, hence him being closest to the door. When the teacher noticed him being hot she, without drama, moved to be next to him to make sure that she was ready to act if needed.

Pause – the teacher knew that if she reacted in anything other than a very calm manner Philip was likely to 'feed' off her stress and escalate into behaviours that would be difficult for him, her and the other children. She tuned into her own breathing and regulated herself before she started talking to Philip.

Regulate – to help Philip regulate she kept her voice low, she gave him space and removed him to somewhere that was quieter and cooler – then helped him to regulate his breathing.

This teacher was practised in managing Philip's behaviour. It may take you some time to develop this level of skill. Relationship (Chapter Three) was key to the ongoing needs that Philip displayed along with her own ability to regulate and manage her emotions (Chapter Five). Visualising how you might manage a situation like those with Philip or Kyle is a helpful way of beginning to develop your skills.

Once the immediate issue has been managed with the child or young person now calm or no longer in the classroom the safeguarding approach is not yet complete.

Understand – when the child or young person is calmer try and spend some time with the child or young person to understand what might have triggered the behaviour in the first place. Depending on your involvement with the child or young person it is preferable for this to be done after the lesson without other prying ears however it may have to be done quietly later in the lesson. Develop your own hypotheses and test these if the child or young person is unable to identify or communicate verbally what the issue is. Be careful not to have a hypothesis that you are reluctant to let go if the child or young person talks about something that is totally different from that which you expected.

This is also the opportunity to try to work out the underlying need that has prompted the behaviour. Use the skills that you developed in reading Chapter Four.

Accept – when you are speaking with the child or young person after the incident make sure that you make it clear that you have separated the behaviour from what you think about the child or young person. In Chapter Three, we saw how self-esteem or self-worth is a key part of the child or young person's ability to make and maintain relationships. It is also a key element in being able to manage one's own behaviour. A child or young person who has been abused is likely to have low self-esteem as well as poor self-management or regulation skills. They need to know that you still hold them in high regard in order to feel safe and to accept that the way that they have behaved might not have been very helpful. We will return to this when we talk about shame in Chapter Seven.

Repair – many schools have now adopted a restorative justice approach. Even if the school that you are working in does not do this formally you can implement it in your practice. Restorative justice can be defined as a process that brings those harmed by crime or conflict and those responsible for the harm into communication, enabling everyone affected by a particular incident to play a part in repairing the harm and finding a positive way forward. (Restorative Justice Council, n.d.)

In supporting a child or young person who has become dysregulated and therefore possibly hurt other children, young people or adults and have doubtless disrupted learning you need to help them to determine how they can put things right. This might be by tidying up the mess they have made, apologising to those they have hurt, having some time out to think about what they have done (sometimes through 'detention') or a more formal restorative process. For 'repair' in a safeguarding approach it is vital to make sure that the trigger is addressed before this happens as the child or young person is unlikely to be able to make retribution if they still are not assured that their unmet need has been recognised and that they are safe. They need to build trust first before they can be vulnerable enough to take part in any restorative process.

Supporting Children or Young People to Regulate

We can all become dysregulated from time to time, however in general children or young people learn to regulate from their parents when they are small babies and develop these skills over time so that during their school journey they become more and more proficient in learning how to respond to social cues and regulate effectively. As we have seen and will explore further in Chapter Seven, children or young people who have experienced abuse or other traumatic situations are likely to have experienced a significant 'impact on the developing nervous system, which can lead to impairment in the capacity to relate and to emotionally self-regulate' (Howard, 2016 p25). For a child or young person in your class(es) it is important for you to understand how their previous experiences may have impaired their neurological development so that you can teach them the skills they need to learn how to manage their emotions. Without this learning a child or young person who has experienced abuse will struggle to learn and progress with their academic development. Some children or young people with safeguarding needs may have been fortunate enough to have had another teacher who understood their experiences, built relationship and worked to support the development of regulation skills, others may not. Irrespective of this you will need to know what the issues are that the child or young person is subject to and work on the development of relationship before you can build regulation.

In the case study for Philip we saw how his teacher helped him to regulate. She had spent some time working with Philip to understand what was going on at home. This had been reported to the Designated Safeguarding Lead (DSL) and a social worker was working with the family under a Child in Need (CIN) Plan (see Chapter Two for more information about these). While this was helping to support Philip at home it had not addressed the regulation difficulties he was experiencing as a result of the abuse. His teacher had talked to Philip to help both him and her identify what the precursors were to his dysregulated behaviour so that she could spot these in the moment and support co-regulation to prevent a full scale 'melt down'. She had also worked with him to develop strategies that he felt comfortable with to enable regulation. Philip was not a 'natural hugger' (Ferguson, Kelly and Pink, 2022 p13) so he had asked for space to be able to leave the classroom and they had practised breathing together to bring down his heart rate. The first few occasions they had tried this out in real time Philip had taken a considerable amount of time to return to a regulated state; however, time they had become more practiced. The result is a calm morning where other children were able to learn.

This might seem like a lot of time and effort. Consider, however, what it might have been like had she not spent this time. There may have been a more Kyle-like incident – a disrupted class, an injured member of staff, the Head Teacher being involved and a dysregulated pupil running from school. Dysregulation tends not to be a one-off event either, so multiply that by regular incidents and you can see how spending time and effort in developing a strategy, alongside Philip was sensible use of time.

In both Kyle's and Philip's case studies the term 'flip his lid' was used. This was deliberate as it is a phrase taken from a technique that can be very useful for conceptualising the process of dysregulation called 'Emotion Coaching' (Gilbert, Gus and Rose, 2021). In this technique the brain is imagined as a closed fist, with the thumb tucked in – operating at its full potential with the prefrontal cortex connected to the emotional parts of the brain (more detail of this in Chapter Seven). When we become dysregulated you can imagine the fingers 'flipping' all at once as though the lid has flipped off the brain – disconnecting the thinking part of the brain. The image that is created by doing this helps us to understand what is happening when children and young people are not able to manage their feelings.

There are no easy shortcuts in this process, particularly for child or young person who finds trust hard as a result of their experience of abuse or trauma. Time and consistent persistence will eventually promote behaviour change. Don't lose heart and make sure that you look after yourself during the process so that frustration and disappointment do not derail the work that you are doing – see Chapter Five for support with this.

Case Study 6.4

Background

Hanna had been sexually abused as a child by her father. A series of different schools during her primary schooling had contributed to her struggling to engage with her peers socially as well as having violent outbursts as a result of unregulated trauma. Her underdeveloped ability to interact with others often

(Continued)

resulted in bullying behaviour towards others – calling them names until she got a reaction. A bright child, Hanna often suffered with being bored in class – something she struggled to manage. This frequently led to her leaving the classroom loudly and chaotically (shouting, pushing past chairs and swinging her bag around). She had learnt not to trust adults so was difficult to reach; this led to her being rude to adults particularly when she felt indignant and that she had been treated unfairly.

What Happened?
The school she attended had a sanction-led policy and her behaviour regularly resulted in detentions where she had to sit in silence. This only served to make her angry and alienated her further from both her peers and the staff in the school. Hanna's mother and stepfather were very supportive of the fact that Hanna had experienced something incredibly damaging as a young child and as a result felt that they could not put boundaries in place at home despite her 'bullying' behaviour with her younger half siblings. Teachers in the school felt that Hanna was choosing to behave in these ways and that she was much better able to regulate herself than she did. Hanna was a tall girl and often mistaken for a much older pupil, thus exacerbating the view that she was more capable than she was.

Reflective Questions
- What do you think Hanna's behaviour was communicating?
- How did Hanna show that she was dysregulated?
- What do you think you could do to support Hanna with the needs her behaviour was communicating?
- What safeguarding issues can you identify?
- How might you apply this case study/learning with the children and young people that you work with?

Other Behaviours

So far we have looked at behaviours that happen in the moment as a result of safeguarding issues that have been experienced historically or are being experienced currently. There are, of course a range of other behaviours that you may come across which are more embedded, also caused by the experience of abuse and trauma. Let us have a look at some of these here, with the help of Geddes (2006) and think about what the child or young person might be trying to communicate.

Behaviour as a Result of Attachment Disorder

In Chapter Seven, we will explore attachment further and what you can do to support children and young people with this particular type of difficulty in more detail. Attachment disorder is often a result of neglect, both emotional and physical so it is linked closely with safeguarding and what you might see in your classroom. Some of the behaviours that you might see that communicate attachment difficulties are as follows:

- Avoidantly attached pupils might refuse to complete tasks or even sometimes destroy their own work.
- Ambivalently attached pupils might try to absorb the attention of the teacher in order to manifesting in attention seeking behaviour. As Ross Greene (2014 p12) says 'We all want attention' he goes on to suggest that a child or young person presenting with this sort of behaviour 'lacks the skills to seek attention in an adaptive way'. They might also be underachieving and communicating through behaviour due to inconsistent language development.
- Disorganised attachment pupils might have real difficulty in trusting that the adults and environment around them are secure or safe. They are likely to respond with survival behaviours.

Many of the behaviours that you will see in the classroom will look like the attachment disorder behaviours above. Make sure that you do not automatically assume that they have a disorder – this can only be diagnosed by a qualified professional. However, it is again useful to think about what this behaviour is communicating – often 'I am scared' or 'I am worried' whether the child or young person has attachment issues or not.

> ### Reflective Questions
>
> Think back to the case studies in this chapter:
>
> - Do you think Kyle, Philip or Hanna are showing signs of behaviour that might be linked to attachment issues?
> - If so, what type of attachment issues do you think they might have?
> - What sort of learning might meet the needs they have as a result?

What Else?

As you become more experienced as a teacher you will come across a huge range of behaviours – some of which we have covered in this chapter. It is impossible to cover every behaviour that children and young people will demonstrate. In each situation it is important to remember that 'Kids do well if they can' (Greene, 2014 p11). If you follow this advice, it leads you to explore what children and young people are trying to say with their behaviour. Whether what they are saying demonstrates that they have a safeguarding need which they need your help with or that they need your help to develop the skills to behave in a way that enables them to engage in learning in your classroom (Greene, 2014).

Many schools are now applying a 'trauma informed' approach alongside the 'relational policies' we discussed in Chapter Three and the Restorative Justice techniques we have mentioned in this chapter. These approaches have at their heart the need to recognise the experiences of children or young people and respond accordingly. This will be developed more in Chapter Seven.

Bias in Our Understanding of 'Behaviour Is Communication'

In understanding what children or young people are trying to say to us through their behaviour, it is important not to make assumptions. We all do, so we need to challenge these both for ourselves and others that we work with. We should not assume a child or young person is aggressive because he has experienced domestic abuse like Kyle. We should not assume a child or young person is unkind to others because she has experienced sexual abuse like Hanna and we should not assume that a child or young person is behaving in a certain way because of their cultural, religious or ethnic background nor because of their LGBTQ + status. Let's have a look at a few examples and see how this can happen so that you can think about how to challenge both your own thinking and that of others.

Case Study 6.5

Background

Ellie had socially transitioned at school but was having a hard time at home. Despite having given permission for Ellie to socially transition her parents were not able to accept Ellie as she now was and this caused significant stress and upset. Ellie often presented in school as quiet and there were days when the arguments at home meant that she was unable to engage in learning.

What Happened?

Ellie became more withdrawn at school and appeared to look very tired, even falling asleep in some classes. Her form tutor had spoken to her parents on numerous occasions so when he was told that Ellie had fallen asleep in class he felt that this was likely because of the angst at home linked to Ellie transitioning.

When Ellie fell asleep in her physics lesson again her form tutor thought he had better just check in with her and find out if there was anything else worrying her. He started the conversation by asking how things were at home. Once Ellie had explained that nothing had really changed he then asked if there was anything else she wanted to tell him. They had a good relationship as it was her tutor who had helped her break the news to her peers that she would be transitioning. It was likely this strong relationship that encouraged Ellie to tell her tutor that she had met someone online and that they were in a 'relationship'. This male was in the United States so they were often online together till late at night. Ellie's tutor asked more questions and became worried about the nature of the relationship and the duration of the late night calls. He told Ellie that he was worried for her and that he needed to tell the DSL so that they could decide how to make sure that she was safe. Ellie was really worried about what her parents would say. Her tutor reassured her that everyone wanted her to be safe and that she would be involved in the decision-making going forwards even if the adults had to act in a way that she didn't like.

The DSL decided to ask Ellie's parents into school. They held a meeting and Ellie attended with her tutor to support her. They encouraged her to talk about the online partner. The adults were able to separate their worries about the online risk from the difficulties Ellie was having with her parents over transitioning. As a result, Ellie agreed for her mother to 'meet' the online partner. This resulted in the discovery that the partner was not who he said he was and also not the age that he had stated. Ellie realised that she was being groomed and the individual was reported to the police.

Reflective Questions
- How did Ellie being 'trans' mean that the abuse she was experiencing was almost not spotted?
- What safeguarding issues can you identify?
- How might you apply this case study/learning with the children and young people that you work with?

Summary for This Chapter

In this chapter, we have looked at how abuse, trauma or safeguarding needs might be communicated through a child or young person's behaviour. We have explored how you might help children and young people reconnect with the thinking part of their brain to enable you to work out what their behaviour is telling you. We have thought about self-regulation techniques and restorative processes that help a child or young person who has been behaving in a way that has disrupted their own or others learning to return to a state where they can access education effectively.

References

Felitti, V.J., Anda, R.F., Nordenberg, D., Williamson, D.F., Spitz, A.M., Edwards, V., Koss, M.P. and Marks, J.S. (1998) 'Relationship of childhood abuse and household dysfunction to many of the leading causes of death in adults. The Adverse Childhood Experiences (ACE) Study', *American Journal of Preventative Medicine*, 14(4) pp. 245–248.

Ferguson, H., Kelly, L. and Pink, S. (2022) 'Social work and child protection for a post-pandemic world: the re-making of practice during COVID-19 and its renewal beyond it', *Journal of Social Work Practice*, 36(12) pp. 5–24.

Geddes, H. (2006) *Attachment in the Classroom*. London: Worth.

Gilbert, L., Gus, L. and Rose, J. (2021) *Emotion Coaching with Children and Young People in Schools: Promoting Positive Behaviour, Wellbeing and Resilience*. London: Jessica Kingsley Publications.

Golding, K.S. (2015) 'Connection before correction: supporting parents to meet the challenges of parenting children who have been traumatised within their early parenting environments', *Child Australia*, 40(2), pp. 152–159.

Greene, R.W. (2014) *Lost at School*. New York: Scribner.

Howard, J. (2016) 'Rethinking traditional behaviour management to better support complex trauma-surviving students', *International Journal on School Disaffection*, 12(2), pp. 25–44.

Restorative Justice (n.d.) https://restorativejustice.org.uk/what-restorative-justice#:~:text=Restorative%20justice%20brings%20those%20harmed,wider%20field%20called%20restorative%20practice [Accessed 2.9.23].

Siegel, D. and Byson, T.P. (2015) *No Drama Discipline*. London: Scribe.

7

Emotionally Sensitive Strategies

> **Chapter Aims**
>
> - To understand trauma.
> - To understand trauma-informed and shame sensitive practice.
> - To understand Adverse Childhood Experiences (ACEs).
> - To develop an understanding of attachment.

Introduction

This chapter explores trauma, trauma-informed and shame sensitive practice alongside attachment awareness and the concept of Adverse Childhood Experiences often referred to as ACEs (Felitti et al., 1998). We look at how these theories can be implemented in classrooms in order to support children and young people who have experienced abuse or damaging experiences. Linking closely to Chapter Six, this chapter explores the emotions of children and young people who have experienced challenges in their lives, looking at brain development and consequential classroom implications.

Trauma

Since soldiers in the First World War were first diagnosed with 'shell shock' there has been a medical and psychological interest in trauma. The development of trauma as a discipline in its own right, however, has been more recent – through the 1990s in particular.

What Then, Is Trauma?

Bessel Van der Kolk is one of the most influential researchers and writers in the field of trauma. He details the rediscovery of trauma through his work with Vietnam veterans. He describes trauma as not just being 'an event that took place sometime in the past', he says 'it is also the imprint left by that experience on the mind, brain and body' (Van de Kolk, 2014 p21). He tells us that 'this imprint has ongoing consequences for how the human organism manages to survive in the present' (Van de Kolk, 2014 p21). Gabor Maté in his work suggests that trauma is not what happens to you, it is what happens inside you as a result of what happens to you (Maté, 2015). While 'The UK Trauma Council' (n.d.) on their website defines trauma as 'the way that some distressing events are so extreme or intense that they overwhelm a person's ability to cope, resulting in lasting negative impact'.

What these definitions and many of the others have in common is that trauma is an internal response to a distressing or difficult event. So, we can begin to see how trauma and safeguarding are intrinsically linked. Any child or young person who has experienced abuse has lived through a potentially traumatic experience. While they are not necessarily synonymous you will have seen in this book and you will see in school that abuse, safeguarding needs or issues and trauma as terms which are often used fluidly.

What Does Trauma Do to the Brain?

The part of the brain responsible for emotional responses to events is the limbic system. It controls the fight, flight, freeze, fawn or flop responses in the brain as we explored in Chapter Six. This part of the brain sits between the cerebral (prefrontal) cortex and the brainstem. The prefrontal cortex is sometimes called the thinking brain and is what is needed for intellectual development (academic learning) and decision-making – it can only be engaged if other parts of the brain, specifically the limbic system, are operating effectively.

The limbic system contains the thalamus and hypothalamus which control, for example, the regulation of thirst, hunger and mood. The basal ganglia responsible for reward processing, habit formation, movement and learning is also involved in the actions of the limbic system. With these three areas we can already see how a child or young person who has experienced a distressing event might exhibit some of the behaviours we see in school. For example, a child or young person who drinks a lot or is unable to accept praise and reward.

In addition to the thalamus, hypothalamus and basal ganglia, there are two other major structures in the limbic system; the hippocampus and the amygdala as illustrated in Figure 7.1.

Amygdala

The amygdala is involved in emotional behaviour, in our responses to feelings like pleasure, fear, anxiety and anger. It attaches emotional content to memories of events. It is particularly key in the processing of fear. When the amygdala is activated during a traumatic experience, it interferes with how that memory is stored in the hippocampus. This might lead to a memory being fragmented, affecting recall and the ability to articulate the memory.

A child or young person who has experienced trauma may process fear differently in the amygdala, triggering a survival response in what might seem to be an unfrightening situation.

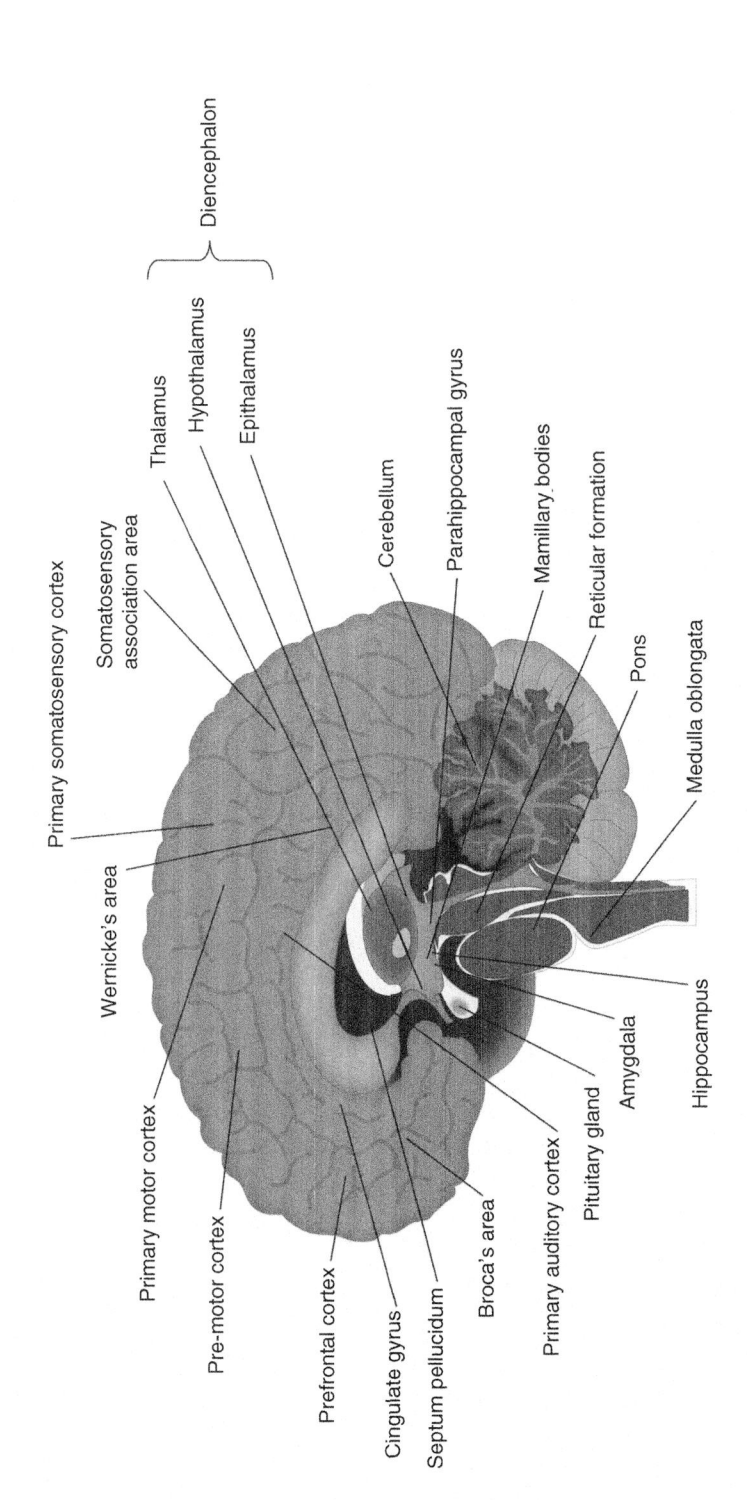

Figure 7.1 The Limbic System and Other Parts of the Brain

Hippocampus

The hippocampus is the memory centre of the brain responsible for laying down long-term memories created in other parts of the brain. It is where our memories are associated with various senses. So you can see how a child or young person who has experienced a trauma might associate a certain smell with a traumatic or frightening event consequentially being triggered if they experience the smell without the trauma.

The hippocampus is also responsible for the making of new cells called neurons which are important for learning through one type of the brain plasticity process. An understanding of this neuroscience is key to understanding how trauma, abuse and neglect is affecting the developing brain and what this might mean for the behaviour and learning of the children or young people in your class or classes.

Case Study 7.1

Background

Sian was often tired at school and struggled with learning right from the start. Her older brother had already been permanently excluded from school for what was described as challenging behaviour. Her mother had grown up in care and her father, who had recently moved out of the family home, was also care experienced. Social care had been involved with the family on and off for a number of years.

As Sian progressed into Key Stage Two she had been on the special needs register for mild learning difficulties for two years and her behaviour became increasingly 'difficult' meaning that she often refused to do the work that she was being supported to do and would leave the classroom and hang around either in the playground or the corridor refusing to go back into the class.

Sian's teacher noticed that she often came to school in clothes that had not been washed. She also often told her teacher that she was hungry and the class teacher noticed that she ate her school dinner speedily, always took extra bread and anything else she was offered. There were times that Sian's teacher noticed that Sian's breath smelt and she sometimes smelt of urine. Sian noted all of these on the school online safeguarding management system and asked to see the school's Designated Safeguarding Lead (DSL) to discuss her concerns. The DSL asked the class teacher to continue to monitor how Sian presented and to continue to support Sian in a trauma-informed way, building the relationship with her.

On one occasion, the school called Mum to see if she could persuade Sian return to lessons. Sian had crawled under a table and refused to come out. The class teacher eventually coaxed Sian out and encouraged her back into class.

What Happened?

Sian had not attended school for a few days. Although the attendance officer had phoned Mum who had said Sian was ill the class teacher was still concerned, Sian was never absent. The class teacher had been continuing to monitor her concerns after the previous discussion with the DSL and this absence raised alarm bells for her. She made sure that the DSL knew about the current absence and her concerns for Sian.

The DSL and the attendance officer went to the family home. They discovered Sian running round the house in just a vest, there was a pile of dirty clothes on the kitchen floor obscuring the washing machine. The counter tops were piled high with plates, empty pizza boxes and a cat litter tray. They asked if they could go upstairs. The bath was full of bedding that smelt strongly of urine and both Sian and her brother's beds were broken.

The DSL made an immediate referral to social care who visited the house before the end of the day and made arrangements for Sian to be cared for under and emergency care order. Sian was back in school the following day. She had to be interviewed by a number of professionals to find out what life was like for her at home. The DSL acknowledged that the class teacher knew Sian best and therefore was the best person to support Sian through this.

Reflective Questions

Sian was clearly suffering from harm (see Chapter Two)

- What category of harm was she suffering from?
- Do you think Sian was communicating or showing that she was suffering from trauma? If so, how?
- What did the class teacher do to help identify the child protection issue?
- What else did the class teacher do to support Sian with what she was experiencing?
- How might you apply this case study/learning with the children and young people that you work with?

What Is Trauma-Informed Practice?

The government produced a working definition of trauma-informed practice in November 2022. In it they describe trauma-informed practice as an approach 'which is grounded in understanding that trauma exposure can impact an individual's neurological, biological, psychological and social development' (UK Government, 2022 n.p). In school we can think of a trauma-informed approach in the following terms:

> Trauma informed education is an evidence-based approach with benefits including improved attendance, academic achievement, emotional regulation, confidence and relationship building. (Emerson, 2022, p 356)

How Can You Develop a Trauma-Informed Classroom?

A trauma-informed approach includes the following:

- Safety – both physical and emotional
- Trustworthiness – consistent and persistent expectations
- Choice – enabling the victim of trauma to take control
- Collaboration – ensuring the sharing of power over what happens
- Empowerment – developing skills and resilience for the future
- Cultural consideration – moving past stereotypes and biases to respond to an individual's needs

    Adapted from Wilson, Pence and Conradi (2013) and UK Government (2022)

You will see that we have already considered trustworthiness in Chapter Three and we will cover safety in Chapter Eight.

Choice

Ensuring that your classroom offers children and young people the opportunity to make choices will teach them how to make choices safely. Having this type of agency over what happens is key to those who are suffering from a trauma or shame (which we will define later in this chapter) response. Being able to have some control over what happens can help mitigate the feelings of helplessness that can often be a symptom of their experiences. For example – can children and young people choose how they will present their learning? Can children and young people choose where they sit? Can children and young people choose how they contribute to class?

Collaboration

This links closely to 'choice'. Children and young people and young people who have experienced trauma often exhibit behaviours that can be experienced as challenging (as we explored in Chapter Six) and as such are not children and young people who are asked to collaborate or contribute to aspects of their own provision and that of the school in general. Providing opportunities for children and young people to co-design their own learning/environment or how to approach the learning will enable them to learn about agency and how to think about the future. Collaborating with you and any other adults in the classroom will help them to understand that adults are there to support their lives not just make all the decisions.

Empowerment

Teaching children and young people implicitly and explicitly about resilience or fortitude, strength building and what their rights are leads to them becoming empowered both in their lives now but also for their futures. We will explore this in more detail in Chapter Ten.

Cultural Consideration

Many of our children and young people have different cultural norms and perceptions to us. In understanding trauma, we need to acknowledge that gender, sexual orientation, age, religion, disability, race or ethnicity can be the cause of traumatic experiences. These are all protected characteristics under the *Equality Act* (UK Government, 2010) which is one of the statutes that underpins *Keeping Children Safe in Education* (DfE, 2024). Ensuring that we are responsive to these traumas in the same way as other traumas is vital in our approach. It is particularly important that we ensure trauma is not caused in our classrooms through behaviours that single out a child or young person because they are perceived to be different. These behaviours can often be minimised by those who carry them out but are termed 'micro aggressions' and can be damaging, there is more about this in Chapter Eight.

Case Study 7.2

Background

Abraham was just starting to teach whole classes on his teaching practice. He wanted to adopt a trauma-informed approach as he had learnt about it through his undergraduate degree. He had talked to the class teacher and his mentor about how he could introduce some practices into his class to support everyone's learning and to particularly support Freddie who was on a child protection plan for neglect and often had challenges in adhering to the class rules and accessing the learning.

What Happened

In the first lesson that Abraham taught he asked the class what they wanted as the boundaries – telling them that he preferred this word to the word rules. He also asked them to think about how they would like to present the learning he was going to ask them to do, giving them three options that they could choose from. He had planned that this would only take a small part of the lesson but found the young people in his class were really engaged in discussing this. With Abraham's support they thought about some options for the boundaries and made sure that everyone, including Freddie, agreed to them. They also had a vote about how the work was going to be presented.

During Abraham's teaching practice the young people in the class were motivated to learn as they had chosen that they would produce a poster about their learning. They, generally, worked hard to think about the content and the key points. Freddie managed to engage with his group most of the time having been allowed to choose who he worked with. When he found it challenging Abraham adopted the language of choice asking Freddie what he needed to be able to adhere to the boundaries he had agreed to and to re-engage with the learning. While this did not work all of the time, Freddie was successful in contributing the group poster and engaged in the learning more frequently that he had previously.

(Continued)

> **Reflective Questions**
> - How did Abraham go about changing the approach in the classroom to use trauma-informed practice?
> - What do you think the safeguarding issues are for Freddie?
> - Do you think that you would be confident to implement a different approach in the class/classes that you work with?

Shame Sensitive Practice

More recently there has been further development in the understanding of trauma-informed practice. As has already been pointed out not everyone will experience an event as traumatic, while others will experience a wider range of events than identified in the ACEs (Felitti et al., 1998) study as distressing. This has led to some researchers suggesting that shame is a more ubiquitous emotion which everyone suffers from at some point in their lives. Defined as 'a negative self-conscious emotion; an experience that arises when we are concerned about how we are seen and judged by others' (Dalzeal and Gibson, 2022 p3). Post-traumatic shame responses can lead to behaviours which are often seen in schools – avoidance, isolation, detachment, confrontation and so on (Dolezal and Gibson, 2022). Children and young people who have experienced abuse or neglect will often feel shame as a result of their experiences. Perhaps feeling as though what they have suffered is their fault in some way.

The experience of shame, particularly for a young brain may result in the survival behaviours we explored in Chapter Six as the child or young person responds to protect themselves. Shame can therefore become a barrier to accessing learning just as trauma can. Alongside trauma-informed approaches, Dolezal and Gibson (2022) suggest that we need to adopt a shame sensitive approach. They think that this approach is threefold:

Acknowledging Shame

We should understand what causes children and young people to feel shame. Understanding how shame affects our own thinking, actions and behaviour is important in acknowledging what happens in a classroom environment. This means that we should not ask directly what makes a child or young person feel shame, just as we should not ask what traumatic experiences they have had.

There are times when you will know that a child or young person has felt shame or might have felt shame. For example, think about how a child or young person might feel about re-entering a classroom where they have been dysregulated (see Chapter Six). It is important to recognise this and support that child or young person to overcome the feelings so that shame does not get in the way of accessing learning.

Avoiding Shame

Everyone working in school should be aware of how shame is often caused when there is a power differential, such as adult to child or young person. The adults should think about their language, demeanour, questioning style and emotional expression to prevent causing children and young people to feel shame. This is particularly important if a child or young person has chosen to speak to you about something that has happened to them (see Chapter Four).

Keeping Children Safe in Education (Department for Education (DfE), 2024) articulates how humiliating children and young people is considered to be a low-level concern (see Chapter Two). Humiliation is a shameful experience and should not come from you as a class teacher. Think about, for example how it feels to have your grades or scores read out in front of others in the class if you have done badly. Think about the effect of a sarcastic comment about how a child speaks or dresses or looks. Think about how a child might feel to be reprimanded in public. As a class teacher you do not want to be the cause of shame and the possible consequential behaviours.

Addressing Shame

Understanding the children and young people in our class is key to a trauma-informed and a shame sensitive approach – this links closely to Chapter Three and the relationships that you build. Understanding how the experience of shame is felt is important in addressing the feeling. This helps children and young people to express those feelings in a way that does not prevent their learning.

> ### Case Study 7.3
>
> In Chapter Six you were introduced to Kyle. The episode where he 'flipped his lid' and ran from school.
>
> #### Background
> The following day Kyle returned to school but was reluctant to even come inside the building. The teacher who had been in the classroom the day before went out to greet Kyle, with a genuine smile. She talked to him quietly, telling him that she understood what had happened yesterday and did not blame him for how he responded. She asked if there was anything that he needed in order to return to the class. Kyle told her that he was embarrassed for all the other class members to be looking at him when he walked in. He also did not want to explain why it had happened. The class teacher asked if he would like her to ask the class to carry on working when Kyle came in. She also asked if she could explain that Kyle had had a difficult experience at home and that they should be sensitive to how he felt without asking him about it directly. He agreed to this and the teacher went back
>
> *(Continued)*

into the classroom agreeing he would come in when she indicated to him that she had spoken to the rest of the class.

What Happened?
The class were receptive to the class teacher's explanation and expectations about their behaviour towards Kyle. Kyle was able to 'slide' into the back of the class. The class teacher asked the teaching assistant to work with Kyle to help him catch up on the learning that he had missed.

Reflective Questions
- How do you think Kyle's teacher's behaviour helped him to return to the classroom?
- How might you apply this case study/learning with the children and young people that you work with?

Adverse Childhood Experiences (ACEs)

Earlier in this book and this chapter we have referred to ACEs. The Adverse Childhood Experiences (ACEs) study (Felitti et al., 1998) explored the relationship between childhood abuse and household dysfunction and negative outcomes for adults, particularly with regards to health and employment. This study revolutionised the approach to those who had suffered trauma as children and young people and has been replicated many times over. In the United Kingdom many organisations including local authorities and schools adopted an ACEs-aware stance. You may find that staff in the school you work in use ACEs interchangeably with trauma. It is useful then to understand what came out of the ACEs study and how it supports you in your classroom practice and how it has been critiqued.

ACEs are described as highly stressful, and potentially traumatic, events or situations that occur during childhood and/or adolescence. These are usually categorised from the original study as the following: physical, sexual or emotional abuse, emotional or physical neglect, mental illness, substance misuse, an incarcerated relative, domestic abuse and parental separation. As you can see the list contains some of the child abuse and safeguarding issues we covered in Chapter Two. As you can also see it doesn't cover many of the other safeguarding issues that we covered and that are listed in *Keeping Children Safe in Education* (DfE, 2024). So, while it is a useful way of conceptualising the experiences of children and young people, it is not comprehensive and should not be treated as such. It must also be noted that the original researchers published a more recent article in 2020 cautioning against the use of a tick list approach to assessing whether a child, young person or adult has experienced an ACE (Anda et al., 2020). A number of schools have adopted this approach. It fails to acknowledge the trauma children and young people might experience as a result of other issues. Some schools have even conducted training where staff have been asked to complete their own questionnaire. If this happens to you make sure that you take care of yourself (Chapter Five) and others – you are well within your rights to refuse to complete such a task.

Attachment

In Chapter Six you were introduced to attachment issues. Our relationships with our parents are thought to account for our development, personality and outcomes throughout our lives. This relationship has been conceptualised as 'attachment'. If a child or young person has experienced disruption in that relationship or abuse within that relationship it is likely to have an effect on their ability to engage with school and with others.

Introduction to the Concept of Attachment

In the middle of the twentieth century, scientists began to try to explain how parenting influences us. From noticing that geese imprint on a mother figure to orphaned baby monkeys thriving with a terry cloth feeding bottle, they explored what this might mean for humans. John Bowlby is commonly accredited with developing 'Attachment Theory' to explain how infants develop an internal working model that forms the basis of all subsequent relationships. This was further developed by his colleague Mary Ainsworth (Ding and Littleton, 2005).

A key aspect of attachment theory is that children and young people learn from early relationships with, as Bowlby suggested, a mother figure and as a result build up a set of expectations about themselves in relation to others. This is the internal working model (IWM). Later research focused on a significant adult rather than just a mother figure. While the mechanism for the neurological development of attachment is complex, Olson and Cozolino (2014) explain it as follows:

> the relationship with the primary caregiver causes some networks of neurons to connect, while other networks do not have a chance to grow in the fragile, developing infant brain. This creates deeply established core brain structures, carrying patterns of relationship that persist into adulthood. (Olson and Cozolino, 2014 p60)

While some of our relationship patterns persist, Bowlby suggested that our attachment models are not permanent and can be changed. He felt that relationships could be established with other consistently and reliably available adults that influence how we continue to develop. This presents opportunities for teachers and the relationships that we develop with children and young people (Chapter Three).

Ainsworth went on to identify different three different types of attachment: secure, insecure and absent. Further sub types of insecure attachment, avoidant, anxious or ambivalent and disorganised or disoriented attachment, were subsequently identified.

While it is possible to recognise the type of attachment we have by the age of one (Olson and Cozolino, 2014) most of us will not have attachment styles which cause ongoing challenges with relationship development. However, some of the children and young people that you work with will. Without a formal diagnosis, however, it is impossible to say that children, young people or even adults are suffering from 'attachment disorder' (Ding and Littleton, 2005). We can however recognise behaviours that a child or young person might demonstrate as a result of attachment issues (Chapter Six) and respond in a way that demonstrates attachment awareness (Bombèr, 2015). It might also be useful to think about whether you have a particular attachment style and whether that influences your approach to your relationships, particularly those with children and young people.

What Is Attachment Aware Practice?

Bombèr (2015), in her Attachment Aware School Series, describes how attachment awareness begins with an

> understanding that security, through the experience of safe and attuned relationships, is necessary for every pupil to be able to settle to learning and make the most of all the educational opportunities out there. It is only when a pupil's attachment system is attended to that their exploratory system can really come into play. (Bombèr 2015, p1)

Both Bombèr (2015) and Geddes (2006) suggest that providing a reliable and secure base is the foundation for good practice here. This clearly links back to relationship as explored in Chapter Three, a nuanced understanding of what a child might be experiencing and how to respond to those feelings. If a child or young person does have a formal diagnosis they should be having some therapeutic support however you will need to think about what you do in the classroom. It is even more important to explore ideas as to how to approach attachment aware practice in your classroom for those who have not received a diagnosis but whose behaviour suggests that they may have attachment issues. If you are not sure what is already in place for a child or young person then make sure that you talk to the DSL or the Special Educational Needs Coordinator (SENCO) to clarify. The following ideas for what you can do in your classroom are adapted from Geddes (2006):

Avoidant Attachment – Pupils Who Can't Ask for Help

Children and young people with avoidant attachment are likely fearful of close proximity and often of the learning task. If you are teaching a child or young person with a diagnosis of avoidant attachment or you suspect this as a result of their behaviour (Chapter Six), then you will need to work hard to build a relationship that provides a bridge between their innate anxiety about relationships and tasks and the fact that you, as the teacher, need to support them with their learning. Work with the child or young person to resolve how close they need to sit to you in class so that they feel supported without having to ask. Think about providing learning activities that are carefully scaffolded with support material that can be easily accessed. Boundaries and structured activities with concrete expectations and outcomes can also be helpful. It may also be that peer working is a useful way of mediating the difficulties that children and young people with avoidant attachment have with the proximity of adults.

Case Study 7.4

Background
Martyna had experienced a difficult childhood and was now in year 8. She had moved a lot as she lived with different family members. Her Mum had significant mental health issues and had not been around for most of her early life, her Dad had struggled to care for a young baby so Martyna had first been cared for by her elderly grandmother and when she had struggled she was then cared for by two aunties spending time with both of them. She was now back living with both her Mum and her Dad but had struggled to build a relationship with either of them.

Martyna's history teacher noticed that Martyna would often not complete any work in class even when she had checked that Martyna understood and had encouraged Martyna to ask for help.

Martyna's teacher asked the DSL if there was anything she should know and was told the background. The DSL said that other teachers had noticed the same thing and that he was concerned that Martyna had undiagnosed attachment issues. The history teacher asked if she could try some strategies.

What Happened?
The history teacher spoke to Martyna and asked if she had any particular friends in the class. The two girls she identified were asked to sit next to Martyna and it was agreed between them all that if Martyna was struggling that she would speak to them and one of them would alert the teacher. The history teacher also asked if Martyna could think of anything that was preventing her from working or if there was anything that she thought would help her with the work without her having to ask the teacher. After the conversation the history teacher noticed the three girls chatting. At the end of the lesson one of Martyna's friends gave the teacher a list of things that they had come up with that would help Martyna, including a request for bank of starting phrases that would help Martyna get going.

The history teacher was able to put together the bank of starting phrases and found that this not only helped Martyna but also some of the other young people in the class.

(Continued)

> **Reflective Questions**
> - Why do you think the DSL felt that Martyna was experiencing undiagnosed avoidant attachment?
> - What do you think the safeguarding issues are for Martyna?
> - How might you apply this case study/learning with the children and young people that you work with?

Anxious/Ambivalent Attachment – Pupils Who Fear Separation

Children and young people with ambivalent attachment are likely to keep close to adults in order to prevent the fear or anxiety of separation. If you are teaching a child or young person with a diagnosis of ambivalent attachment or you suspect this as a result of their behaviour (Chapter Six), then you will need to think about how to make sure that they are assured of your presence without spending all your teaching time with them. This could be assuring them that you will be back to support them in a specified amount of time while they undertake a task which is broken down into small manageable steps. The child or young person needs to know that you are keeping them in mind – this can be achieved by them having something that reminds them of you on their desk or by engaging them from across the classroom. Facilitating their support of peers or leading groups can also direct their need to be in charge of relationships in a more positive way.

> ## Case Study 7.5
>
> ### Background
> Charlotte was in Reception. She was very clingy and refused to leave the teacher's side. She was cared for by a foster carer as her parent's drug taking had meant that they were unable to take care of her. She had been in the care of one foster carer for the first six months of her life and then had to be moved. Charlotte's teacher knew this background from her induction with the DSL where he had asked if there were any children in the class that he should know about.
>
> ### What Happened?
> The teacher decided to give Charlotte a timer which had a picture of his face stuck to it. He said to her that when the sand ran out then she could come and find him and he would give her some time and then they would start the timer again.
>
> Charlotte slowly learnt to be on her own or with other children in the class for the period of time that the timer was going. Her teacher had to remind her a lot to begin with. Once she had mastered the first timer the teacher substituted it for a longer one and then a longer one again. By the end of the Spring term, Charlotte had learnt that she did not need to be with the teacher all the time and when she did go and find him he was able to give her focused attention.

Reflective Questions
- Why do you think that Charlotte was experiencing symptoms of anxious or ambivalent attachment?
- What do you think the safeguarding issues are for Charlotte?
- How might you apply this case study/learning with the children and young people that you work with?

Disorganised/Disorientated Attachment – Pupils Who Find School/Life Particularly Hard

Children and young people with disorganised attachment are likely to have an inconsistent response to relationships and therefore can be particularly difficult to reach in the classroom. If you are teaching a child or young person with a diagnosis of disorganised attachment or you suspect this as a result of their behaviour (Chapter Six), then you will need to prioritise safety, reliability and predictability. For these children and young people 'love' is often not enough and physical containment might be necessary to substitute for not being psychologically held. They are likely to have experienced the most extreme lack of brain development of all those with attachment disorder, resulting in brain pathways dominated by fight and flight so that connections to the prefrontal cortex are limited and learning is likely to have been delayed. Understanding this and working with the school's SENCO is vital to support the learning and behaviour of these children and young people.

Case Study 7.6

Background
Sammy had experienced a very difficult start in life. He had experienced domestic abuse in his pre-verbal development stage, a period of homelessness, living in care and then returning to live with his Mum who could be volatile. He had struggled with mainstream education and developed a fight response when he could not cope. He was educated in a special school as a result of his needs.

What Happened
Sammy was agitated in class despite the fact that he was with a teacher and teaching assistant that he liked. One of the other children in the class responded to something that the teacher said by laughing really loudly. This caused Sammy to jump up, rush over to the child and hit him. The class teacher reached the two young people and held Sammy in an approved hold. He then removed Sammy from the classroom and stayed with him while he calmed. He knew from previous incidents that Sammy liked to remain in the hold to help him calm down. The teaching assistant remained in the classroom and ensured that the other child was not badly hurt and that the other children in the class were safe.

(Continued)

Sammy was able to calm down but was not sure what had caused him to react in the way that he did. The class teacher spoke to the DSL and SENCO about the incident and then recorded it on the school's online record system. All three of them made sure that they tracked the incidents of Sammy's behaviour to use this for future planning and support for Sammy.

Reflective Questions
- Why do you think that Sammy was experiencing symptoms of disorganised or disoriented attachment?
- What did the teacher do that helped Sammy to calm down?
- What do you think the safeguarding issues are for Sammy?
- How might you apply this case study/learning with the children and young people that you work with?

The Link to Maslow

What you have seen in this chapter is how you can use various tools and theoretical approaches to ensure that children's basic needs, as defined, by Maslow (1943) (see Figure 7.2) are met. Remember that everyone needs to have at least the first four levels fulfiled if they are going to learn effectively. Use what you have learnt so far to ensure that those children with safeguarding needs have an equitable chance of achieving in your classroom by you and your colleagues ensuring that basic needs are met through trauma-informed, shame sensitive and attachment aware approaches.

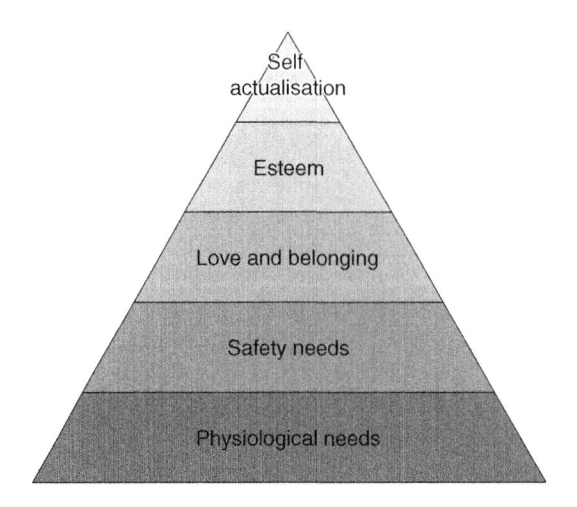

Figure 7.2 Maslow's Hierarchy of Needs (after Maslow, 1943)

Summary for This Chapter

In this chapter, we have explored the theoretical concepts of trauma, shame and attachment. We have also looked at the research that established what ACEs (Felitti et al., 1998) are. We have looked at how this links to basic needs as conceptualised by Maslow (1943). Alongside this we have looked at how schools can provide a trauma-informed, shame sensitive and attachment aware approach to support children and young people who have experienced abuse or have safeguarding needs. How you can apply this in your classroom has been explored through the use of case studies.

References

Anda, R.F., Porter, L.E. and Brown, D.W. (2020) 'Inside the adverse childhood experience score: strengths, limitations, and misapplications', *American Journal of Preventive Medicine*, 59(2), pp. 293–295.

Bombèr, L.M. (2015) *Attachment Aware School Series*. Belper: Worth Publishing.

Department for Education (DfE) (2024) *Keeping Children Safe in Education*. London: DfE. Available at https://www.gov.uk/government/publications/keeping-children-safe-in-education-2 [Accessed 26.5.24].

Ding, S. and Littleton, K. (2005) *Children's Personal and Social Development*. Oxford: Blackwell Publishing.

Dolezal, L. and Gibson, M. (2022) 'Beyond a trauma-informed approach and towards shame-sensitive practice', *Humanities and Social Sciences Communications*. https://doi.org/10.1057/s41599-022-01227-z [Accessed 17.9.23].

Emmerson, A. (2022) 'The case for trauma-informed behaviour policies', *Pastoral Care in Education*, 40(3), pp. 352–359.

Felitti, V.J., Anda, R.F., Nordenberg, D., Williamson, D.F., Spitz, A.M., Edwards, V., Koss, M.P. and Marks, J.S. (1998) 'Relationship of childhood abuse and household dysfunction to many of the leading causes of death in adults. The Adverse Childhood Experiences (ACE) Study', *American Journal of Preventative Medicine*, 14(4), pp. 245–248.

Geddes, H. (2006) *Attachment in the Classroom*. London: Worth.

Maslow, A.H. (1943) 'A theory of human motivation', *Psychological Review*, 50(4), pp. 430–437.

Mate, G. (2015) *The Body Says No*. London: Vermillion.

Olson, K. and Cozolino, L. (2014) *The Invisible Classroom*. New York: W. W. Norton and Company.

UK Government. (2010) *Equality Act c. 15*. London: HMSO. Available at: https://www.legislation.gov.uk/ukpga/2010/15/contents [Accessed on 26.4.24].

UK Government (2022) *Working Definition of Trauma Informed Practice*. https://www.gov.uk/government/publications/working-definition-of-trauma-informed-practice/working-definition-of-trauma-informed-practice [Accessed 2.9.23].

UK Trauma Council (n.d.) https://uktraumacouncil.org/resources/childhood-trauma-and-the-brain [Accessed 2.9.23].

Van der Kolk, B.A. (2014). *The Body Keeps the Score: Brain, Mind, and Body in the Healing of Trauma*. New York: Penguin Random House.

Wilson, C., Pence, D.M. and Conradi, L. (2013) *Trauma Informed Care*. Encyclopaedia of Social Work. Available at: https://doi.org/10.1093/acrefore/9780199975839.013.1063 [Accessed 26.3.24].

8

Creating a Safe Environment

> **Chapter Aims**
>
> - To explore what it feels like to feel safe.
> - To learn about what happens in the body when we feel safe.
> - To think about how to create physical, emotional and psychological safety in the classroom and for parents and carers.
> - To think about Equality, Diversity and Inclusion and how this relates to creating a safe environment.
> - To explore why this is important for safeguarding.

Introduction

We can all think of places that make us feel safe and cherished. The challenge is how to do this in a class environment. This chapter explores some of the theory relating to creating safe spaces and options for how you can create a safe classroom where all children and young people flourish and thrive and those with safeguarding needs, trauma or abuse are able to learn.

The Neurobiology of Safety

Much of what we do in school is based in theory and understanding of what happens to us as we grow, develop and learn. This is an understanding of neurology which also includes the other elements of our complex nervous systems which is made up of our central nervous system – including the brain and the spinal cord. One of the key elements of this system is the autonomic nervous system (ANS) which is 'central to our experience of feeling safe' (Olson and Cozolino, 2014 p16). This ANS operates below the level of consciousness and links to all the major organs. If the system is activated it therefore can raise heart rate, cause shortness of breath or upset an individual's stomach. All these neurobiological events are involved in the trauma responses explained in Chapter Six and as a consequence of brain responses explained in Chapter Seven through the sympathetic nervous system one of the ANS's three subsystems. The other two subsystems are two branches of the parasympathetic system, the ventral vagal and the dorsal vagal. The ventral vagal operates when we feel safe and enables us to be calm and learn. The dorsal vagal overrides all the systems, if the feeling of danger escalates to unmanageable levels – this is when we see the flop trauma response. All three of the systems within our ANS are 'profoundly responsive to our environment, including the internal state of those around us' (Olson and Cozolino, 2014, p16). Remember in Chapter Five the importance of looking after our own CNS was mentioned – we need to feel safe as much as the children and young people that we teach.

In their book *The Invisible Classroom*, Olson and Cozolino (2014) refer to 'the neurobiological and human connections' (preface) as the entirety of the collection of physical, emotional and psychological connections which enable us to help children and young people feel safe and therefore influence learning.

Trauma-Informed Practice

With an understanding of what is going on inside children and young people's bodies let's pick up some of the unexplored theory about trauma-informed practice that we discovered in Chapter Seven. As you read, Wilson, Conradi and Spence (2013) and government guidance (UK Government, 2022) identified six aspects to consider in providing a trauma-informed environment. The first of these was safety: emotional, psychological and physical.

Why Is Trauma-Informed Practice Important to Children with Safeguarding Needs?

As we have already explored children, who have been abused, neglected or have safeguarding issues going on in their lives are likely to have experienced trauma. This can result in the visible challenges as we have seen in Chapter Six and the invisible ones both in the brain (Chapter Seven) and, in the introduction, to the neurobiology of safety. A trauma informed approach is a useful methodology to support a safe environment in your classroom. It also contributes to the relationships you are encouraged to build in Chapter Three. It supports understanding that behaviour is communication (Chapter Six) and encourages children not only to feel safe enough to speak up about what is happening to them (Chapter Four) but also to be able to concentrate and focus on their learning.

> ### Reflective Questions
>
> - How do you know when you don't feel safe?
> - Where do you feel safe?
> - What makes that place feel safe?
> - Do you have any memories of feeling safe at school? If so, what do you think helped you to feel safe there?
> - How might the answers to these questions help you to create safe classroom.

Let's now look at what you can do to create an emotionally, psychologically and physically safe classroom.

Emotional Safety

This can be provided by not being afraid to let children know that they are liked and cared for (Chapter Three). It is also provided by us feeling emotionally safe ourselves – checking that we are not reacting to things in our own lives or in the classroom that might influence the atmosphere for children and young people (Brummer, 2020).

Emotional safety can specifically be created by making sure that you are kind (Chapter Three) and welcoming to the children and young people that you teach. If they sense negativity they will feel unsafe. This sense is communicated predominantly through non-verbal signals from your face, voice and body. Work on making sure that you communicate positively through smiling, a relaxed voice tone and body language. This is hard if you are stressed or not managing your own emotions which is why it is so important to look after your own well-being as we explored in Chapter Five. The calming rituals we explored are also important for the emotional safety of the children and young people in the classroom. Some teachers have successfully introduced mindfulness while others have routines that help children or young people to calm and settle, such as collecting of resources, music, introductory or settling activities.

Research also tells us that the presence of resilience promoting relationships or opportunities to develop fortitude in their lives is a key factor in supporting children and young people to cope with and recover from adverse experiences (Daisely, 2022). As we have already found out boundaries need to be in place and there needs to be clear expectations for children and young people as this contributes to their feelings of safety. Make sure that the boundaries you create are fair, equitable and conform to the school's approach to behaviour so we can be 'firm on behaviour and kind on the child' (Trauma informed Schools, n.d. n.p). If this does not fit with your personal values around managing children or young people, then you will need to question whether this is the right school for you in the long term. If you don't feel emotionally or psychologically safe then you are unlikely to be able to maintain a safe learning environment for the children and young people that you teach.

Case Study 8.1

Background
Jack was having a hard time at home. His older brother had been arrested. The men he had been hanging around had visited his home to ask for what they referred to as their possessions that Jack's brother had been keeping for them. This made Jack feel unsafe at home and in the area around his house. Jack's parents were finding it difficult to come to terms with what Jack's brother had been involved with and as a result they were not emotionally available for Jack.

(Continued)

What Happened?

Jack arrived early for his art lesson. The art teacher welcomed him with her usual smile and asked him to help her set up the equipment for the lesson without asking any other questions. Jack quietly got on with helping her to set up for the lesson and then got out his sketch book and started drawing. After the lesson Jack hung back and helped to tidy up. The art teacher asked Jack if he was all right as he had been particularly quiet in the lesson. Jack broke down and explained what was going on at home. The art teacher explained that she would need to pass this on the Designated Safeguarding Lead (DSL) but that Jack could ask her to spend time in the art room whenever he needed if things got too much.

The DSL rang Jack's parents and sensitively suggested that they talk about how Jack felt and what they and the school could do to support both Jack and the rest of the family during what was clearly a difficult time.

Reflective Questions

- What do you think it was about the art room and the art teacher's attitude that Jack found safe?
- What safeguarding issues can you identify in the case study?
- How might you apply this case study/learning to your work with children or young people?

Psychological Safety

Psychological safety, a concept explored by Amy Edmondson (2019) examining its relationship to team learning and performance, is as relevant to classrooms as it is to the business environment that she first applied it to. Psychological safety means an absence of interpersonal fear. Edmondson (2019) suggests that when psychological safety is present, people are able to speak out. This 'felt safety' should be embedded within the culture of the school – psychological safety is established by governors and senior leadership in the first instance. Whether there is a whole school approach or not, if you are able to provide a psychologically safe environment, then children and young people will be able to tell you about what is going on in their lives and perhaps the lives of their friends.

This psychological safety can be established through creating a classroom environment where children or young people are not scared to speak to you or any of the other adults. Where children or young people can make comments about learning or anything else and are not ridiculed by others in the room, adults or other pupils. You need to ensure that any sort of humiliation by other pupils is swiftly quashed without shaming those who do it. Ensuring that children and young people who are unkind to others in your presence understand that it is not acceptable will mean that those looking for a safe place to disclose are more likely to feel comfortable to choose you. This means having a clear and fair approach to managing and hopefully resolving any bullying or other forms of child-on-child abuse. If you do not do this, children or young people might not feel safe to speak out in your classroom and maybe will not disclose at all.

Children and young people who need to tell someone about difficulties they are experiencing often 'try out' the adults around them with something minor in the first instance to see how that adult responds – whether that adult does as they say they will or whether they do anything at all. All of these 'subliminal' actions tell children and young people that your classroom is a safe space.

Psychological safety is something that you are only aware of if it is not present or when you think about it in retrospect. Think of your own experiences where you have felt psychologically safe or not. If you felt safe did you think about it at the time?

Other Aspects in Creating Safe Learning Environment

In Chapter Five, we looked at well-being and the research of Sue Roffey (2012); here we will pick up what she says about creating a safe learning environment in the arena of psychological safety in addition to ensuring that children and young people are confident that bullying behaviours are addressed and as a result reduced.

Making mistakes

Children and young people need to know that it is all right to make mistakes. This unequivocally supports their academic learning and can be modelled by you and other adults in the classroom. It has an even more significant use in the support of safeguarding – for children and young people who have something to disclose in particular. These children and young people, while also experiencing abuse and trauma, often feel that what has happened to them is their fault. If mistakes are not acceptable in your classroom, then they will be cautious of 'admitting' something that might have huge consequences. For these children and young people, in particular, knowing that things can go wrong, they can be put right or be resolved and restoration happen can be life changing. Feeling safe around mistakes starts with you making sure that when children and young people make learning mistakes these are understood and then scaffolded to ensure success next time. When you make a mistake, acknowledge it and put it right without being embarrassed or belittling yourself – no saying 'silly me'.

Case Study 8.2

Background
There had been a number of incidents of young people getting hurt in the school where Steve was teaching physical education. There was a group of young people that were suspected of carrying out the incidents but there was no evidence to support the suspicions.

(Continued)

With all the classes that he taught Steve had made it clear that they could make mistakes and that they needn't be scared to try new activities. In his Year 9 gymnastics lessons he had further encouraged this by demonstrating something that he told the students that he had never accomplished before. When it didn't work he asked them to critique what he had done wrong and make suggestions for what he could do to improve.

What Happened?

At the end of one of his lessons a couple of girls from the class asked if they could talk to him. They explained that they were scared to walk to their next class from the PE lesson as they had to go past a stairwell at the far end of the school where there were no cameras. They explained that this was where a group of students were often to be found and they were scared of what might happen to them. Steve offered to walk that way on his way to his next lesson on the field so that he could disperse anyone who was in the stairwell. He also told them that he would have to pass on what they had said to him. He told them if it was at all possible he would make sure that the group of students that they were scared of would not find out that they had spoken to him about them.

Steve moved the group of students on when he walked past the stairwell and then made sure that he spoke to the Assistant Head with responsibility for behaviour what he had seen and what he had been told.

A rota was drawn up to make sure that the stairwell was supervised during break times and lesson transitions until a camera could be installed. The students who had been 'hanging out' there were spoken to and one of them admitted to being the 'perpetrators' of harm to the other young people in the school. The incidents of young people being hurt stopped.

Reflective Questions

- What do you think it was about Steve's approach that made the girls feel safe enough to talk to him about their fears?
- What safeguarding issues can you identify in the case study?
- How might you apply this case study/learning to your work with children or young people?

Physical Safety

Children and young people need to know they are safe from outside influences but also, they can get out should they need to. Sometimes physical safety will be giving a child or young person a hug or holding them – make sure you know and are comfortable with your school policy on this. In Chapter Six, we met Philip and his teacher. She had ensured that his desk was close to the door so that if he was triggered to be dysregulated she could encourage him to leave the room with the minimum of drama. Some children will not want to be close to the door or to a window and may even want to be in the most inaccessible chair in the classroom.

Make sure you know the children or young people you are teaching well so that you can support them with these needs as well as learning needs. For some children or young people knowing that they have a particular chair in the classroom will help them feel calm and therefore able to learn.

Other things that contribute to physical safety that you may need to consider are how cold or hot is the room. Does a particular child need to have air? There are also design elements that you can consider – what colours are calming? What is the lighting like? How comfortable is the furniture? Many of these are particularly vital for children and young people with a diagnosis or suspicion of neurodiversity but also for those children you have suffered abuse, neglect or trauma. You may not have the opportunity to influence these but you can add plants or back walls to improve the aesthetics and provide physical or environmental safety cues for the children and young people your classroom or classrooms.

In addition to the physical location of children in the classroom you need to think about how the classroom feels. Many schools have fantastic displays and busy working walls to support learning. Also, with the pressure on teachers, there is often little time to tidy and organise learning spaces. Add this to communal spaces that are sometimes crowded and loud, spaces in school can often feel overwhelming. We need to stop and think how does an environment in my classroom affect children or young people? Busy environments can contribute to body and brain stress, often acting as a trigger for those who have suffered trauma or shame as we saw in Chapters Six and Seven. What can you do to ensure that the classroom or classrooms you are teaching in, and the teaching you have planned, enables children or young people to feel physically safe?

Case Study 8.3

Background

Maryam was a refugee. She had fled her own country in the midst of war and bombing with her family. She had arrived in a new country and a new school where she was learning a new language alongside the fact that she was not going to witness her new best friend being killed in a bomb blast as she had experienced before she had to flee.

The year five teachers were planning a spectacular start to the World War II topic, one that they had used before. They were going to simulate an air raid by playing air raid warnings while getting the children to hide under the desks. Then they were going to play the sound of airplanes overhead with bombs being dropped.

Maryam's teacher was uncomfortable about this approach this year because of Maryam's experiences but didn't want either Maryam or the other children to miss out on learning experience that had been very successful in the past. He went and

(Continued)

asked the advice of the Designated Safeguarding Lead (DSL) who was overseeing the support for Maryam and her siblings who were also in the school. He suggested a meeting with himself, the year five teachers and Maryam's Dad who spoke good English to decide what would be the best way forward.

What Happened?

Maryam's Dad felt that Maryam was strong enough to decide for herself if she wanted to take part in the activity. The class teacher and the school's Emotional Literacy Support Assistant (ELSA) who knew Maryam best talked to her – giving her the opportunity to hear the sound track beforehand to see how it made her feel. Maryam wanted to hear the sound track and once she had said that she felt that she could manage the activity and did not want to be left out.

The class teacher made sure Maryam and her family knew when the activity was due to take place, while the DSL made sure that the school's ELSA was allocated to year five for the duration of the activity and that Maryam knew that she could seek that support if she needed it.

Reflective Questions

- What do you think was worrying Maryam's teacher?
- What would do you think would have happened if the activity had gone ahead without any thought or planning?
- How did the teacher and others make sure that this activity was physically safe for Maryam?
- What safeguarding issues can you identify in the case study?
- How might you apply this case study/learning to your work with children or young people?

Going Outside

In Case Study 5.4 we saw Stephanie take her class outside. Being outside can act as a naturally calm and soothing space – particularly if you are lucky enough to have green spaces in your surroundings. If you can use the outdoor space to sooth the collective central nervous systems, then both the children or young people and you will benefit.

Movement

Being able to move is another really easy way to help soothe the collective central nervous systems. Children and young people who have experienced abuse or trauma are often, as we saw in Chapter Six, trapped in freeze response. One way to release this is to encourage positive movement. It is also really helpful for other children and young people in the class as it aids concentration in the long run.

Pupil Voice

In thinking about creating a safe environment, it is useful to harness pupil voice, particularly that of those who may have experienced trauma. As you saw in Case Study 8.3, engaging children, or young people, in the decision-making process often leads to results that we don't expect. This supports the Trauma-Informed Practice model explained in Chapter Seven. So, what do the children or young people in your class or classes think? What do they feel? What do they want their classroom to look and feel like? How often do they want to go outside? What sort of movement helps them to focus? This will be more complex for those of you who have a high turnover of pupils in your classroom, or where you teach in multiple classrooms, but it is possible. A whole school approach helps.

When you are asking children and young people about how they would like the classroom to be, use the terminology we have explored here, particularly that around psychological safety. Remember that you don't recognise psychological safety unless it is absent. If you have a number of children or young people who identify this as a feature it is something to follow up to ensure that there are not spaces in which they do not feel safe. It might mean that you have been able to identify an issue that has not been recognised up to now –either at home or outside the home (contextual safeguarding – see Chapter Two) and Case Study 8.2.

Equality, Diversity and Inclusion

When you are considering how you make your classroom a safe space for everyone it is important to consider all those children who are considered different. Many suffer from 'the impacts of trauma including homophobia, racism, classism or sexism' (Brummer, 2020 p 12). While being different does not necessarily mean you have been abused or have experienced trauma it does make you more vulnerable to abuse from bullying and microaggressions. The Oxford Dictionary defines microaggressions as:

> a statement, action, or incident regarded as an instance of indirect, subtle, or unintentional discrimination against members of a marginalised group such as a racial or ethnic minority. (Oxford Dictionary, n.d. n.p.)

It is important that in your classroom these and other 'attacks' on children and young people who are different by virtue of being considered as being a person with a protected characteristic as defined by the *Equality Act* (UK Government, 2010) or who consider themselves to be neurodiverse. Many of children and young people who are different will have experienced the trauma of being singled out in a negative fashion, may have been abused as a result of their difference or may have experienced systemic abuse. Your classroom should be a safe space where all these things are considered to ensure that everyone is safe.

Parents and Carers

Olson and Cozolino (2014) suggest that 'developing a culture of safety can even have a positive effect on parents' or carers' interaction with the school' (p44). Your relationship with parents and carers is an important one whatever phase of education you teach in as explored in Chapter Three. Providing a safe place for parents or carers to talk about their hopes and fears for their children is vital to building this relationship. Depending on where you teach you may find that a number of the parents or carers of children or young people that you teach had a negative experience of school. The neurobiology of adults responds in the same way as the children and young people in your class or classes. Being relaxed, smiling and ensuring that you do not give off a sense of judgement will help their ANS to sense safety. Add to this your treatment of their children or young people and you will be well on your way to providing as safe environment for them.

Case Study 8.4

Background
One of the science teachers in the department that Stanley was teaching in was giving extra tuition to young people who had not done very well in their mock GCSEs. One of the young people receiving this tuition – Jane – was in Stanley's class. Stanley had met with her mother after the mocks and had been in touch regularly to talk about Jane's progress and reassure her that Jane was going to get the grades she needed to go on to study A-levels.

What Happened?
Jane's mother phoned school and asked to speak to Stanley urgently. She told Stanley that the teacher who was tutoring Jane had sent Jane a social media request on Instagram which she had accepted and now Jane was being exposed to pictures of the teacher semi-dressed. Despite how Stanley felt he responded calmly to Jane's mother and asked her to come to the school with the phone. He then went immediately to the Head Teacher and asked him to take over the management of what Jane had told him.

The Head Teacher phoned the Local Authority Designated Officer (LADO) who arranged a strategy meeting. The LADO asked that the Head Teacher remove the science teacher from the school while the police investigated.

Stanley took over Jane's tutoring and made sure that he only communicated with Jane in class and anything else was managed via phone calls and emails (via his school email account) to Jane's mother.

Reflective Questions
- What do you think it was about Stanley's approach that meant Jane's mother felt that she could disclose to him?
- What safeguarding issues can you identify in the case study?
- How might you apply this case study/learning to your work with children, young people or their parents or carers?

Summary for This Chapter

In this chapter, we have looked at how you might think about creating a safe space in your classroom or classrooms not only for learning but also for those children or young people who are looking for a place where they can safely disclose what is happening to them. We have thought about movement and the use of outside spaces in creating this safety. We have explored how you can involve children or young people in decisions about both the space and the learning to ensure that their trauma or abuse issues are not exacerbated or 'triggered' something in the environment or learning. We have also looked at how you can work on ensuring that parents and carers feel safe too.

References

Brummer, J. (2020) *Building a Trauma-Informed Restorative School: Skills and Approaches for Improving Culture and Behavior.* London: Jessica Kingsley Publishers.

Daisely, B. (2022) *Fortitude: The Myth of Resilience, and the Secrets of Inner Strength Teas.* Cornerstone Press.

Edmondson, A. (2019) *The Fearless Organisation.* Hoboken: Wiley.

Olson, K. and Cozolino, L. (2014) *The Invisible Classroom.* New York: W. W. Norton & Company.

Roffey, S. (2012) 'Pupil wellbeing-Teacher wellbeing: Two sides of the same coin?', *Education and Child Psychology*, 29(4), pp. 8, 17.

Trauma Informed Schools (n.d.) Available at: https://www.traumainformedschools.co.uk/ [Accessed 17.2.24].

UK Government (2010) *Equality Act c. 15.* London: HMSO. Available at: https://www.legislation.gov.uk/ukpga/2010/15/contents [Accessed on 26.4.24].

UK Government (2022) *Working Definition of Trauma Informed Practice.* https://www.gov.uk/government/publications/working-definition-of-trauma-informed-practice/working-definition-of-trauma-informed-practice [Accessed 2.9.23].

Wilson, C., Pence, D.M. and Conradi, L. (2013) *Trauma Informed Care.* Encyclopaedia of Social Work. Available at: https://doi.org/10.1093/acrefore/9780199975839.013.1063 [Accessed 26.3.24].

9

Early Help – What Does This Mean for You?

> **Chapter Aims**
>
> - To define what early help is.
> - To think about what teachers can look for and their role in an effective early help/early intervention structure.
> - How to build effective partnerships with parents and others to support children and their families.
> - To explore how to use an early help assessment tool.

Introduction

Spotting issues before they result in harm is key to safeguarding culture. *Keeping Children Safe in Education* (Department for Education (DfE), 2024 p9) says that 'All staff should be aware of their local early help process and understand their role in it'. On page ten there is then more detail about what to look out for. In this chapter, we will explore local early help processes and the additional detail a little further giving more detailed explanations so you can be clear what ***you*** are required to do. Remember that each school has to publish their own offer of Early Help which, as a part of the whole school safeguarding team, you will be part of delivering. Make sure when you meet with the Designated Safeguarding Lead (DSL) during your induction that you are clear what their expectations are of you. This is explored in more detail in Chapter One.

Local Early Help Processes

What *Keeping Children Safe in Education* (DfE, 2024) means here is the support that is available from the Local Authority to support children or young people and their families where they do not meet the threshold for Section 47 or Section 17 support. You will remember that we covered these sections of the *Children Act* (UK Government, 1989) in Chapter Two. Where children or young people are not considered to be at risk of significant harm or to be 'in need' they and their families might be offered some other support. This is often a family support or early help worker helping to ensure that routines and boundaries are in place and implemented. There is no standard requirement for how this is managed or assessed; so in order to understand what happens in your locality you can explore your local children's partnership web pages or again you can ask your school's DSL.

The school that you work in might also access early help support from other organisations such as charities or other statutory bodies – there is more detail about these in Chapter One where we look at Multi-agency partners.

Early Help

Keeping Children Safe in Education (DfE, 2024) identifies that any child or young person might, at any point in their life, benefit from some support from an effective early help provision. By this it means providing an 'intervention' to ensure that difficulties a child or young person is facing do not escalate to the level of child protection as described in the *Children Act* (UK Government, 1989). An 'intervention' could be a variety of things – it could be as simple as listening to and advocating for a child or young person. It could be providing advice and guidance to the child or young person's parent or could equally be about making sure that a child or young person is able to access a club or activity outside of school. All of these Early Help 'interventions' are something that you, as a teacher, could provide depending on how your school operates – again make sure that you are clear what your role is in the safeguarding team at your school (Chapter One).

Some of the children and young people who might possibly be in need of this early support to prevent referrals to children's social care are identified in *Keeping Children Safe in Education* (DfE, 2024). So let's have a look at these children and young people, what you might see in the classroom, what types of 'intervention' you might be able to carry out to provide early help in your role as class teacher and when you should talk to the DSL to ensure that a holistic response is managed.

Children or young people who are disabled or have certain health conditions and has specific additional needs and Children or young people who have special educational needs (SEN): These are likely to be children who are on the special needs register and have a My Plan, My Plan+ or an Education Health Care Plan (EHCP). There may be other agencies already involved in their support (see Chapter One). You should know who these children are in the class(es) that you teach so you will not have to guess who they are. Whenever you start teaching a new class you should speak to their previous teacher or the school's Special Education Needs Coordinator (SENCO or SENDCo). When you do this you should ask what behavioural and educational needs the child or young person has and how you should provide for these in your teaching and classroom management. The behaviours are particularly important as any changes might indicate a safeguarding need as we saw in Chapter Six. The strategies that are suggested to you form the basis of the agreed early help; however, this does not prevent you from developing your own relationship with the child or young person (Chapter Three) and therefore a possible unique approach to the child or young person in your classroom. Just make sure that this is not completely at odds with the needs of the child, young person or school. As always, discuss with other staff and make sure that what you are doing is reasonable and effective. As far as safeguarding and child protection goes children and young people who are on the special needs register are more likely to experience abuse (Sullivan and Knutson, 2000) but you should not assume that they need early help for safeguarding unless they make a disclosure (Chapter Four) or their behaviour suggests that they are being abused (Chapter Six).

Children or young people who have a mental health need: These children or young people will have a range of diagnoses and potential issues depending on how much help and support they have already received. Again, you are unlikely to be the first person in school to become aware of the need so make sure that you speak to other colleagues before you do anything other than build relationships (Chapter Three) and treat the child or young person with kindness. Depending on what the child or young person is presenting with there will be some behaviours that you will see and there will be some ways in which you can best support with early help in the classroom. Further information about the mental health of children and young people can be found at https://www.youngminds.org.uk/

Case Study 9.1

Background

Diana loved reading and felt most at home in her English lessons despite being very quiet and hardly ever engaging in class discussions. Her English teacher had worked hard to get to know her and her interests and had often been able to recommend authors or books based on the conversations they had in class. She had discovered that Diana loved early nineteenth century novels and had some really interesting ideas about the feminism therein. One day when Diana was working in class her English teacher noticed some red marks on Diana's wrist. She waited till the end of the lesson and then quietly asked Diana if she was OK. When Diana said that she was fine, her English teacher sensitively pointed out that she had seen the red marks on Diana's wrist and asked what they were. Diana started to cry and told her English teacher that she had no friends and felt lonely and isolated. She said that when she was at home she rubbed her metal ruler back and forth over her wrist to take her mind off how she felt.

Diana's English teacher spoke empathetically to Diana and told her that she would have to speak to the school's Designated Safeguarding Lead (DSL) so that they could decide how to help Diana. She asked what Diana would like to happen and what Diana thought would help her with her feelings. Diana told her teacher that she found it difficult to make friends and that she had been the only one to transfer from her junior school. She said that she had not really spoken to anyone since starting in Year Seven.

(Continued)

> ### What Happened?
> Diana's English teacher spoke to the DSL and suggested that she could run a small reading group for a few weeks. She knew a couple of children in other classes who had similar reading interests and thought they might like to be invited too. The DSL thought this might be a good idea and asked the English teacher to speak to Diana and ensure that she spoke to a member of the safeguarding team who had mental health first aid training.
>
> ### Reflective Questions
> - What do you think Diana's English teacher was worried about?
> - What do you think Diana's English teacher was trying to achieve in through the 'intervention' of a reading club?
> - How was any mental health need addressed?
> - What safeguarding issues can you identify?
> - How might you apply this case study/learning with the children and young people that you work with?

Children or young people who are young carers: These children and young people are under 18 and help to look after a relative with a disability, illness, mental health condition or drug or alcohol problem. Again other colleagues should already be aware of these children so along with asking about children and young people with Special Educational Needs (SEN) and those with known mental health needs you need to check whether there are any young carers in your class(es). Again these children may have a range of needs but in all likelihood school is a place where they can be like their peers and not have the responsibilities that they may have at home. Ensure that you make time to build your relationship with these children and young people and that you are sensitive to issues they might be facing. They could be looking after themselves in a way that may not be expected for their age, shopping for and preparing meals, washing their own clothes and caring for younger siblings. This might mean limited time for their own social interaction, rest, relaxation and almost certainly will reduce what they are able to give in terms of homework. Make sure that you negotiate with other colleagues, and the child or young person and perhaps give them other options in terms of helping them to achieve academically while also accommodating their early help needs.

If you discover a child or young person is caring and it has not been mentioned to you then you should discuss this with the DSL. You also need to be aware that they are more vulnerable to grooming and exploitation particularly online so make sure you are aware of the signs that you might see (Chapters Two and Eleven) and speak to the DSL if you are concerned.

Case Study 9.2

Background
Terry loved playing football – every break time and every lunchtime. He did not like mathematics and really struggled to understand the concepts and apply them. When he moved into Year Ten he had a new maths teacher. This teacher was new to the school and had very strict rules about handing in homework which Terry was not used to. When he did not hand in his homework for the third time in row the maths teacher told Terry that he would have to stay in at break time to complete the work. Terry lost his temper and shouted at the maths teacher, swearing before walking out of the classroom.

What Happened?
Terry went straight to the welfare officer which is where the maths teacher found him. Before the maths teacher could speak Terry pushed past him and out into the playground where his friends were already playing football. The welfare officer intervened and explained to the maths teacher that Terry was a young carer. That he had a disabled older brother and had to help his single mother to look after him, cooking the family meals every night and reading to his brother to help him sleep. Because of this Terry had had to give up playing for his local football team and had no time to himself at home. The family lived in a small two-bedroom home which was largely taken up with equipment to support his brother. Terry had no space to work at home.

Reflective Questions
- Why do you think Terry was so angry when he lost his break time?
- What do you think the maths teacher could have done differently?
- What safeguarding issues can you identify?
- How might you apply this case study/learning with the children and young people that you work with?

Children or young people who show signs of being drawn in to antisocial or criminal behaviour, including gang involvement and association with organised crime groups or county lines plus children or young people who are at risk of modern slavery, trafficking, sexual or criminal exploitation: These are often referred to as issues relating to contextual safeguarding (see Chapter Two). If you find out that this applies to any of the children or young people you are working with you should definitely discuss it with the DSL and follow their advice and guidance in terms of managing these issues in the classroom. This does not mean that you should not treat these children and young people as you would any other. You build relationships (Chapter Three) so that you know if there has been a change in behaviour

(Chapter Six) and whether the situation for them has escalated and further support might be needed.

Children or young people who are frequently missing or go missing from care or from home and children or young people who are persistently absent from education, including persistent absences for part of the school day: While these children or young people should be well known to the DSL or the school attendance lead you may well be the person who notices that they are absent now – particularly if they have absconded during the school day. Make sure that you always take a register for your class and that you report any children as soon as you can who are missing and should not be. In addition to building relationships, making sure that your classroom is a safe space (Chapter Eight) where there is engaging learning will help entice these children to stay. It is likely not a reflection on you if, despite doing all this, these children and young people still go missing.

Children or young people who are at risk of being radicalised or exploited: You will be required to undertake 'Prevent' training (see Chapter Two) to be able to recognise this type of abuse. If you think that a child has already been radicalised or exploited, then you should report this to the DSL. In terms of early help in the classroom for children or young people who are at risk of being radicalised again building relationships is key. Alongside this teaching children and young people how to be critical of information, learning how to interrogate what is put in front of them so that they can make up their own minds is also vital. This should be part of your standard classroom offer of early help as well as an integral part of what you do as a teacher – teaching children and young people to know their rights and think for themselves is one of your most important roles (see Chapter Ten).

Children or young people who have a family member in prison, or is affected by parental offending: These children or young people should already be known to the DSL and again you should know who they are if needed. It may be school procedure that every class teacher does not have this information shared with them. If you find out that a child or young person is affected, then you should let the DSL know and accept that you might not have anything further shared with you. Your offer of early help here is about your general classroom practice which should follow the guidance in the rest of this book.

Children or young people who is in a family circumstance presenting challenges for the child or young person, such as poverty, drug and alcohol misuse, adult mental health issues and domestic abuse: You should also make sure that you know a little about these situations. Here is a very brief summary and signpost to further information so that you can research in more detail if you have children or young people with these sorts of issues in the school that you teach in.

Poverty: Poverty, at the time of writing, affects around 4.2 million children (CPAG, n.d.) – this equates to an average of nine children or young people in every class of 30. While many of these children and young people are well cared for, poverty has been proven to increase the risk of a child or young person being harmed (Bywater, 2015) although what causes this is not well understood there is some evidence of links to the other issues in the title of this section (Innes-Turnill, 2023).

For more information about the effects of poverty:

Child Poverty Action Group (CPAG) https://cpag.org.uk/

Joseph Rowntree Foundation https://www.jrf.org.uk/

Drug and Alcohol Abuse: There are a number of definitions of substance abuse or substance misuse as it is sometimes known. This definition brings together many of the aspects of the condition.

The use of illegal drugs or the use of prescription or over-the-counter drugs or alcohol for purposes other than those for which they are meant to be used, or in excessive amounts. Substance abuse may lead to social, physical, emotional and job-related problems (or school related problems for children and young people) (Adapted from National Cancer Institute definition, n.d.).

There is evidence of increased physical and sexual abuse in families where there is substance abuse (Walsh, MacMillan and Jamieson, 2003). Abuse may be more likely because of the way alcohol affects the way parents, carers or family members behave towards their children or young people. It may also be because it affects parents' ability to protect their children from harm (Laslett et al., 2012).

Parents and carers who misuse substances may also have chaotic, unpredictable lifestyles and may struggle to recognise and meet their children's needs which may result in their children being at risk of harm.

For more information about how substance abuse can lead to child abuse the NSPCC provides a useful starting point: https://learning.nspcc.org.uk/children-and-families-at-risk/parental-substance-misuse#heading-top.

Domestic Abuse: Domestic Abuse can happen to anyone – it does not discriminate. Anyone in your school or personal community can be a victim, including staff members. Being aware of what domestic abuse is, the signs that someone is suffering and what you can do to help is a key skill, not only to support those you work with but to support friends and family too.

Domestic Abuse is now defined by the Domestic Abuse Act (2021) as an incident or pattern of incidents of controlling, coercive, threatening, degrading and violent behaviour, including sexual violence, in the majority of cases by a partner or ex-partner, but also by a family member or carer (womensaid.org.uk)

This law for the first time and included child witnesses of domestic abuse as victims.

For more information about Domestic Abuse and how it affects children the NSPCC website is a good place to start https://www.nspcc.org.uk/what-is-child-abuse/types-of-abuse/domestic-abuse/

If you read this and think that you are a victim of domestic abuse you can get help from the police or the National Domestic Abuse helpline 0808 2000 247.

For children and young people who have experienced or are experiencing any of these issues, just as with those who are young carers, it is important to understand how their experiences at home affect their ability to engage at school. Every child or young person will respond in an individual way to their needs and you need an individual response in turn. While this might seem overwhelming remember that relationship building is the most important tool in your approach, as well as talking to colleagues to understand what works.

> ## Case Study 9.3
>
> ### Background
> Thomas and his younger sister were at after school club when Thomas' class teacher was leaving school. She noticed Thomas' mum walking up the path to collect them. She stopped to have a quick conversation with her as Thomas had had a particularly good day after being quite challenging since she had started teaching the class. She wanted to share Thomas' success that day. When she spoke to Mum she noticed a strong smell of alcohol coming from her.
>
> ### What Happened?
> Mum continued up the path. Thomas' teacher was worried and phoned the out of hours number for the DSL. The DSL was still in school and said that she would go to after school club and ensure that Thomas' Mum was safe to take the children home.
>
> ### Reflective Questions
> - What 'Early help' role do you think Thomas' teacher would have here?
> - What might Thomas' teacher have noted earlier in the day that might have alerted her to an issue?
> - What safeguarding issues can you identify?
> - How might you apply this case study/learning with the children and young people that you work with?

Children or young people who are misusing alcohol and other drugs themselves: If others in school already know that children and young people are experiencing these sorts of difficulties there should already be some sort of management plan or risk assessment to make sure that both they and others are safe in school. Make sure that your early help here follows the guidance in this document. If there is not one, then it would be good to have a conversation with the DSL so that you know how to recognise if a child or young person turns up to your classroom under the influence and what you should do.

In addition to this you can contribute to the education around the misuse of substances to support children and young people to make healthy decisions in their lives – we will cover this in Chapter Ten.

Children or young people in care, who have returned home to their family from care or who are privately fostered: Your early help role as part of the safeguarding team who support these children and young people is to ensure that they are able to effectively access education in your classroom. Providing the necessary safeguarding support by following the guidance in this book but also by knowing what is in the plan for them. This is often called a Personal Education Plan (PEP) and may be funded by additional pupil premium funding. These plans may require particular support in your teaching and relationship so make sure you know what you need to do and how to track the academic or emotional learning that you are responsible for.

Children who are at risk of so-called honour-based abuse such as Female Genital Mutilation (FGM) or Forced Marriage: Your role here is to support these children or young people to engage in their learning and to follow the safeguarding advice in this book. You will need to be particularly alert to children who talk about going away for extended periods of time and where they are going. You should receive training about all these areas of abuse as part of your induction training so that you know what to look for. This is particularly relevant to the issue of FGM where you have a statutory responsibility to report to the police. This is also covered in Chapter Two.

Case Study 9.4

Background

In a geography lesson the children in a Year 4 class were looking at globes. Angelika was pointing to Mali and telling the children in her group that she was going to the country soon with her mother and adult sister. Angelika's class teacher was interested as she had not heard that Angelika was going to be absent from school. She asked Angelika what she knew about the country and why she was going there. Angelika proudly told her that she was going for a celebration and that her older brothers and Dad were not going and that they would be leaving in a couple of weeks' time.

What Happened?

At the end of the day Angelika's teacher spoke to the DSL who decided that they should speak to Angelika's mother or sister. The DSL asked the class teacher to be in the meeting as she knew both Angelika's mother and sister well having taught Angelika for two terms. The following day when Angelika's sister came to collect her, the class teacher asked if she and the DSL could have a chat. The DSL led the conversation and asked questions about what they were going to Mali for. She also asked sensitive questions about whether the sister was a victim of FGM. When the sister admitted that she was the DSL made a call to the police and Children's Services. Angelika was prevented from travelling to Mali. When it became clear that no one had explained to Angelika the class teacher, as the professional with the closest relationship, was asked to have a conversation with Angelika about what the professionals had been worried about. The DSL coached the class teacher in the conversation so that she felt confident to speak about such a sensitive issue.

(Continued)

> ### Reflective Questions
> - How confident would you be to identity and address FGM?
> - How would you feel if you were asked to have a sensitive conversation with a child or young person you had a good relationship with? What would you do to prepare for it?
> - What safeguarding issues can you identify?
> - How might you apply this case study/learning with the children and young people that you work with?

Building Effective Partnerships With Parents and Others to Support Children and Their Families

Much of building effective partnerships refers back to areas that we have covered in earlier chapters. For example, your role and that of others in the safeguarding team in Chapter One or the work on relationships in Chapter Three. If you can engage with this earlier advice, then you will be able to work with all of those who have a role in providing early help for the children and young people that you teach.

If there is a plan in place to support a child or young person that you teach make sure that in the first instance you follow what is in the plan. If you find that tricky or it simply does not work after you have tried it then make sure you lean on your professional relationships and ask for advice and support. If you find that, having built a relationship with the child, young person or their parent or carer, you want to try a different approach make sure that you discuss this with the DSL or SENCO and parents so that there is an agreed approach. You may have to justify why you want to change what is done for this child or young person so make sure that you have professional or academic evidence to support what you want to do. If your colleagues are not keen for you to try a different approach make sure you ask them to help you understand why they do not think your idea will work and if, ultimately, they ask you not to try a new method then you will have, with good grace, to accept this. If you feel that you need to challenge, you should seek the support of your mentor or a more established colleague to make sure that you are pursuing something that is in the interests of the child or young person.

If you believe a child or young person needs support which is not already in place, then you should talk to other colleagues about how to go about this. In this situation having some ideas as to what might help will probably be welcomed and you can take the initiative in making a difference for that child or young person.

> ## Case Study 9.5
>
> ### Background
> Eddie had diagnosis of autism and had an Education Health Care plan. Most of the time with the support in place, Eddie was able to access the mainstream curriculum and with the exception of a couple of subjects attended lessons with his peers. There were occasions when he became dysregulated and could be aggressive to the adults around him. The plan stated that when this happened the adults were to withdraw and leave Eddie to calm. His class teacher noticed that on these occasions that Eddie took a long time to be ready to return to learning and wondered if there was another way. He had built quite a good relationship with Eddie so after another incident he asked Eddie how the support was going, particularly when he was dysregulated. Eddie said that he felt so sad when this happened because everyone left him and it made him feel bad.
>
> ### What Happened?
> Eddie's teacher decided to speak to the SENCO and suggest a different strategy based on what Eddie had said. The SENCO thought this might be interesting but was reluctant to move away from the agreed strategies without talking to Eddie's parents and she did not have time to schedule a meeting with them for a couple of weeks. The class teacher asked if he could speak to the parents and ask their advice.
>
> The class teacher rang Eddie's parents and told them about his conversation with Eddie. They said that they had noticed that Eddie seemed very sad after incidents of dysregulation at home too. They suggested that they would try a new strategy of staying with him in a safe way at home when this happened and let the class teacher know if it worked. A couple of days later when Eddie's Mum dropped him at school she told his class teacher that the new strategy had worked and that she would call the SENCO and ask for the plan at school to be changed to better support Eddie.
>
> ### Reflective Question
> - What was the class teacher's 'Early help' intervention here?
> - What safeguarding issues can you identify?
> - How might you apply this case study/learning with the children and young people that you work with?

Early Help Assessment Tools

Early help does not have specific statutory guidance so how children, young people and their families are assessed for early help is different wherever you teach. However, there are some parts of any early help assessment that are fairly universal. It is unlikely in the early stages of your teaching career that you will have to complete any sort of early help assessment by yourself. However, if you are the only class teacher or you have become a particular child or young person's key adult as a result of the relationship you have built with them then you may be asked to contribute. Have a look at the questions in the box and think about how you might complete this information for a child or young person you teach.

The only part of safeguarding or child protection that can be carried without consent is a section 47 process (see Chapter Two). So any early help assessment should be carried out with the consent of the parents or carer and if the child or young person is competent enough, their consent too. This can be difficult if the child, young person or family think that the assessment is interfering with their right to a private family life (see Chapter Ten); so whoever is having the explanatory conversation needs to be clear about how the process will support and why the support is needed. This might well be you – if you are the class teacher or the child or young person's key adult. You will probably have, as a result, the closest relationships with the parent (s) or carer (s). This is where you can be key in Early help intervention.

Early help should be a genuinely positive process where everyone is working to make things better for the child or young person. Sometimes, particularly if a referral is being made for early help with another agency a consent form will need to be completed. You might be asked to gain the consent from both the child or young person and a family member if you have the best relationships with them. Make sure you are clear about how early help will support and what it is hoping to achieve.

Possible Early Help Assessment Questions

Home and Family Relationships

- What is the current housing situation? E.g. private rental, any arrears? Is it stable?
- Any significant life events? (death of a family member, house move, new partners)
- Are there family member(s) who struggle with their mental health problems, alcohol or drug dependency?
- Has there been any historical or any ongoing Domestic Abuse?
- Have there been known concerns about child neglect or abuse?
- Home environment – what's good and bad about it?
- Does the child have safe space and what they need to develop?
- What are parent/child/ren relationships like? Warmth? Routines? Consistency? Boundaries?
- How do the child/children behave at home?
- Do you feel you have family members who understand your concerns and who will support you, who are they?
- For the child: Do you like where you live? Do you have your own space? What is your space like?

Work

- Are parents/older children employed? If not, what would help?
- How are you managing financially?
- Are you able to provide for your family's basic needs? What needs to change?
- What aspirations do the adults/older children have?
- For the child: What are your hopes for the future

School/College

- What are the attendance figures for each child/children, is the attendance below 90% – if so why?
- Is the child persistently absent from school/missing?
- Are they achieving academically? What makes it hard to learn? What could help?
- How do child/ren behave at school?
- Triggers of behaviour?
- For the child: How do you feel about school? What are the best and worst bits?

Social/Community

- Are there difficulties which make things worse for you or the child/children, such as neighbour disputes?
- Is there antisocial behaviour or crime impacting your family?
- What support networks do the family have?
- What do you like doing in your spare time?
- Do you have concerns about emerging threats such as criminal exploitation, radicalisation or child sexual exploitation?
- Do you feel safe? Who are your safe people/places?
- For the child: Do you feel safe? Are you engaged in any hobbies? Do you have good friends?

Health and Well-Being

- Are the child/ren clean, hygienic, well fed?
- How often are visits made to the doctor and dentist?
- What do you think about the child's speech, language and communication skills?
- Are there any other additional health needs? Sexual health needs?
- Are there problems for adults about emotional well-being? (Stress, anxiety and self-esteem).
- Are the emotional needs of the child/ren met?
- Are any of the children providing physical or emotional care for a family member due to illness/disability/substance use?
- Are there any caring tasks that pose a risk to the child? Or is the amount/type of care the child is providing impacting, or likely to impact on their health, development, education and social opportunities?

(Continued)

- For the child: Do you have any illnesses, health problems or disability? Who helps you stay healthy? Are there things that make you feel angry/sad? Who can you talk to?

(Adapted from Oxfordshire safeguarding children's board, n.d.)

Reflective Questions
- How much of these do you think you would know as a class teacher?
- How confident would you be to ask these questions if you were asked to speak to a child, young person or family member?
- How invasive or difficult do you think these questions are?
- What would you do think could be done with this information?
- How might you apply this with the children and young people that you work with?

Summary for This Chapter

In this chapter, we have provided a definition of early help. We have, using the information in *Keeping Children Safe in Education* (DfE, 2024), explored which children and young people might need early help and what you can do in the classroom to support. We have thought about your role in the school and the multi-agency process while also thinking about how you can challenge the status quo in terms of what supports children and young people. We have explored the sorts of questions that are asked in early help assessments – while thinking about how difficult this can be both for the professionals and the children, young people and families involved.

References

Bywaters, P. (2015) 'Inequalities in child welfare: Towards a new policy, research and action agenda'. *British Journal of Social Work*, 45, pp. 6–23.

CPAG (n.d.) https://cpag.org.uk/child-poverty/poverty-facts-and-figures [Accessed 10.2.24].

Department for Education (DfE) (2024) *Keeping Children Safe in Education*. London: DfE. Available at: https://www.gov.uk/government/publications/keeping-children-safe-in-education–2 [Accessed 26.5.24].

Innes-Turnill, D. (2023) 'Child Abuse, the narrative of parents living in poverty: A critical analysis of Parental and Professional explanations of why a child was harmed', *Journal of Social Work Practice*, 37(2) pp. 183–197.

Laslett, A., Room, R., Dietze, P. and Ferris, J. (2012) 'Alcohol's involvement in recurrent child abuse and neglect cases', *Addiction*, 107, pp. 1786–1793.

National Cancer Institute (n.d). Available at: https://www.cancer.gov/publications/dictionaries/cancer-terms/def/substance-abuse [Accessed 10.2.24].

Oxfordshire Safeguarding Children's Board (n.d.). Available at: https://www.oscb.org.uk/wp-content/uploads/2019/07/Oxfordshire-Early-Help-Assessment-2019-Prompt-Sheet.docx [Accessed 16.12.23].

Sullivan, P.M. and Knutson, J.F. (2000) 'Maltreatment and disabilities: A population-based epidemiological study', *Child Abuse & Neglect*, 24, pp. 1257–1273.

UK Government (1989) *UK Government (1989) Children Act 1989, c. 41*. London: HMSO. Available at: www.legislation.gov.uk/ukpga/1989/41/contents [Accessed 26.3.24].

Walsh, C., MacMillan, H.L. and Jamieson, E. (2003) 'The relationships between parental substance abuse and child maltreatment: findings from the Ontario Health Supplement', *Child Abuse and Neglect*, 27, pp. 1409–1425.

Women's Aid (n.d.) Available at: https://www.womensaid.org.uk/information-support/what-is-domestic-abuse/ [Accessed 10.2.24].

10

Teaching Safeguarding to Children and Young People

Chapter Aims

- To explore what the formal safeguarding curriculum should contain including an understanding of children's rights.
- To think about how to implement in informal safeguarding curriculum and how this can be managed irrespective of subject specialism.
- To explore how being a role model can aid the teaching of safeguarding.
- To think about how children and young people can take responsibility for safeguarding each other.

Introduction

A key element of safeguarding which is often under explored is what children and young people need to know and how they are taught about it. This is explored here including how to encourage children and young people to take responsibility for their own safeguarding and that of their peers. The idea of pupil leadership is encouraged with strategies for how this can be introduced in different phases.

The Formal Curriculum

There are a number of places where schools can start in the development of their formal provision for safeguarding education. Whatever phase you teach in you need to know what these are and what children and young people are likely to be learning about. These sources are likely to form the basis of the Relationships and Sex Education (RSE)/Relationships, Health and Sex Education (RHSE)/Personal, Health and Sex Education (PHSE) and Citizenship curriculum as well as supporting the provision for learning about keeping safe through assemblies.

The first source is the statutory guidance for RSE and Health Education (Department for Education (DfE), 2019). This document sets out what children and young people should learn about how they manage themselves in their relationships, what positive intimate relationships look like, what their online relationships should look like and how to keep themselves well. There are of course age-related differences to what needs to be taught and if you are a secondary phase teacher you are unlikely to teach the content of this curriculum unless you are a RSE/RHSE/PHSE specialist or you are asked to take on this responsibility. However, it is useful for you to know what the children and young people are learning in these lessons as it may have an impact on the atmosphere in your classroom or on the relationships you have with those that you teach. It is also useful to know what is being taught and how it is being taught in case a child or young person comes to you as their trusted adult for advice and support. It is important that you are not telling them something that is completely at odds with what they have heard from a colleague. If you do not agree with what they are being taught, then this is something that you should follow up professionally rather than contradicting it to the pupil in the first instance (see Chapter Four on how to have difficult conversations). If this is the case, then it is important to be honest with the child or young person and explain that you are not sure what they have been taught and you will have a conversation with your colleague(s) and get back to them. You may need to support them to keep safe in the meantime –we will cover this later in the chapter.

The second source of information is the guidance for citizenship curriculum (DfE, 2013), which is statutory for all children and young people in the secondary phase. Again – if you are not the specialist teacher for this area or you have not been asked to take on this teaching, then you will not be expected to deliver the curriculum but you should know what children and young people are being taught. The same applies here as it did to RSE/RHSE/PHSE – if you do not agree with what is being taught have the conversation with your colleagues before you directly contradict them to the children and young people.

In addition to the subject specific curriculums which directly teach about issues relating to the safeguarding of children and young people, it is important to explore what you teach in other subject areas. Where can you teach safeguarding through the curriculum? For all ages and stages of the development of children and young people lessons about important or difficult subject matter are more likely to be learnt in the context of other learning. So ask yourself the question – how can you weave important aspects of this key learning into other subject areas. The following table gives some examples for all of the areas of curriculum for you to consider. It is not meant to be a comprehensive coverage of all aspects of safeguarding learning in other subjects – that would be a whole other book – however it gives you an idea of what you can think about (Table 10.1).

Table 10.1 Examples of Safeguarding Teaching Opportunities Across the Curriculum

Curriculum Area	Example of Safeguarding
Art and Design	Teaching Art and Design inevitably leads to discussions about how art makes us feel and how we express ourselves. Children and young people are often more willing to express their feelings creatively. The opportunity to challenge the thoughts behind the creations is vital to exploring feelings and perhaps experiences of abuse or trauma that may otherwise remain hidden. Critical analysis skills are a key part of the art curriculum so encourage children and young people to think about the artist's intent.
Biology	In teaching human reproduction there is huge opportunity to talk about the relationships that exist both between a man and woman at conception but also between the mother and child in utero. This gives rise to opportunities to talk about what safe and happy relationships look like. There are also opportunities to teach about healthy lifestyles in relation to how what we consume or use in or on our bodies affects us.
Chemistry	Chemistry is about elements and how they react with each other. This links closely to the chemical effects of substances such as alcohol and drugs. The innovative Chemistry teacher can draw parallels to how these substances can be dangerous to those who take them.
Design and Technology	In practical subjects such as Design Technology the health and safety teaching provides opportunities for teaching children and young people how to keep themselves safe. Home Economics or cooking can facilitate conversations about healthy eating.
English	In the English curriculum, particularly literature, there is much opportunity to choose books that explore themes relating to safeguarding. Even if you are teaching a text which is determined by the school or the exam syllabus there will be the opportunity to explore human relationships and how they look when they are or are not effective. Critical analysis skills are a key part of the English curriculum so encourage children and young people to think about what authors are intending to get the reader to believe.
Geography	In learning about other countries in the world there is opportunity to talk about how children and young people are treated in other countries and cultures. This can lead to discussions about how children and young people think they should be treated and how they feel they should keep themselves safe.
History	Examining lives from the past presents opportunities to analyse our own lives and current practices. This can lead to discussions about how children and young people think they should be treated now in comparison to the past and how they feel they should keep themselves safe in a way that children and young people in the past could not. Critical analysis skills are a key part of the history curriculum so encourage children and young people to think about what evidence means and how reliable it is.
Languages	Good language learning enables exploration not only of the words used but knowledge and understanding about other countries. This presents opportunities to talk about how children and young people are treated in other countries and cultures. This can lead to discussions about how children and young people think they should be treated and how they feel they should keep themselves safe.

(Continued)

Table 10.1 Examples of Safeguarding Teaching Opportunities Across the Curriculum *(Continued)*

Curriculum Area	Example of Safeguarding
Mathematics	Teaching mathematics enables teaching children and young people to think critically. Are numbers doing what they expect them to do? How do we test to make sure that the rules are true, and so on?
	Many children and young people also perceive mathematics as a difficult subject. The teaching of resilience in order to persevere with problem-solving is key for developing self-worth (see Chapter Three).
Music	Teaching Music inevitably leads to discussions about how music makes us feel and how we express ourselves. Children and young people are often more willing to express their feelings creatively. The opportunity to challenge the thoughts behind the creations is vital to exploring feelings and experiences or trauma that may otherwise remain hidden.
Physics	Physics is about matter, energy and motion. In seeking to understand the world teaching critical skills is vital this then links to the ability to analyse what is in our environment and make judgements about it. This is vital for keeping safe.
Physical education	In teaching Physical Education, you are most likely to be the teacher who sees children or young people in clothes that might reveal bruises, so that is the first thing to be aware of if you are teaching this subject – you will need to learn what is normal to expect and what is concerning.
	Physical Education also provides opportunities to teach about safe touch, relationships and healthy lifestyles.
Religious Education	The treatment of children and young people in the past and in current religions and cultures forms part of the Religious Education curriculum, as does the exploration of moral values and the application of these to relationships. This enables discussions of what children and young people think are right and wrong and provides opportunities for challenging those views when necessary.

Reflective Question

- Think about what you teach and what you have read in terms of how you can think about teaching safeguarding in your subject – what could you do to make sure you include it?

The final place for statutory guidance about what children and young people should be taught about keeping themselves safe is *Keeping Children Safe in Education* (DfE, 2024). This document is very clear about the range of things children and young people should know about and what they should be taught and makes particular reference to online safety which we will touch on briefly at the end of this chapter and explore more in Chapter Eleven. Much of the rest of what is in *Keeping Children Safe in Education* (DfE, 2024) is in the statutory curriculums but there are aspects of this which fall to every teacher, whatever their age or subject specialism. It is how you approach this and what you should teach that we will explore later in this chapter under the heading of informal curriculum.

What Else Should Children and Young People Be Taught?
Rights Education

Teaching children and young people about their rights is key to enabling them to keep themselves safe and is a fundamental tenet of Trauma Informed Practice (see Chapter Seven). The United Nations Convention on the Rights of the Child (UNCRC) was adopted in November 1989 and has been signed up to by 196 countries, with only the United States of America having not ratified it at the time of writing.

As a teacher this convention should not only form a fundamental foundation to how you work in school, it should also be something that you talk to the children and young people about. This does not mean that you have to know all 54 articles in intricate detail but knowing what children and young people's key rights are, is vital. You should ensure that you do not contravene these rights in your provision and that the school that you work in does not contravene rights too. If you think that they are, then you may want to talk to your union or your trusted network (see Chapter Five). You should also be able to explain these key rights to the children and young people that you teach and empower them to use that knowledge to keep themselves safe and promote their development. You can explore the convention and the articles via the UNICEF website (https://www.unicef.org.uk/what-we-do/un-convention-child-rights/). There are a number of articles which refer to the right to family life which are difficult to navigate in the child protection arena in that they are contradictory to the most critical interventions when children or young people are removed from their families for their own safety. There are also a number of articles which refer to particular safeguarding issues that are explored in Chapter Two. The following are the key rights that you should familiarise yourself with in terms of your classroom practice:

Article 2 (non-discrimination) – making sure that children and young people are treated equitably irrespective of their protected characteristics.

Article 3 (best interests of the child) – making sure that all decisions made about children and young people have them and their needs at the heart.

Article 6 (life, survival and development) – in school this relates to children and young people's right to be supported to develop to their full potential.

Article 12 (respect for views of the child) – making sure that children and young people have the right to express their views and that these are considered and taken seriously in anything affecting them.

Article 13 (freedom of expression) and *Article 14 (freedom of thought, belief and religion)* – making sure that children and young people can access any information and then believe and express their thoughts and opinions as long as they are legal.

Article 19 (protection from violence, abuse and neglect) – making sure that children and young people are afforded the protection of the *Children Act* (UK Government, 1989).

Article 28 (right to education) and Article 29 (goals of education) – making sure that all children and young people can access education and that the education they receive develops their personality, talents and abilities to the full.

Article 39 (recovery from trauma and reintegration) – for those who have experienced abuse and trauma that there is support to recover.

You will find all the articles in the summary document linked in the reference list which provides an easy to read presentation of all the rights that apply to the children and young people that you teach (UNICEF, n.d.). When you familiarise yourself with them – think about the safeguarding issues that might arise from not adhering to them.

The Informal Curriculum

If you think back to the rest of what you have read in this book about how you become an effective safeguarding practitioner as a class teacher, you will see that in addition to protecting children from harm you are responsible for children's welfare. Key components of this have been covered in other chapters but are worth highlighting again here so that you can think about how you plan to teach them in your classroom and in your lessons:

Self-esteem or self-worth – how do you ensure that you teach the children and young people that you work with about 'unconditional positive regard' (Rogers, in Burr, 2022 p20)? As well as building your own relationships (Chapter Three) you should take every opportunity to teach and exemplify, enabling children and young people to build this for themselves.

Self-regulation – in Chapters Five and Six, we explored thinking about this key element of both our own behaviour and that of the children and the young people we work with. Again you should take every opportunity to model and teach this to the children and young people that you work with. Making explicit when you have regulated or when they have is an important tool in their learning.

Resilience or Fortitude – Bruce Daisley, in his book *Fortitude* (2022), explores this in detail, distilling down some of the component parts that we can apply in our teaching in order to help children and young people develop this key approach to life and the difficulties it can present. He talks particularly of opportunities to develop the qualities of 'autonomy, competence and relatedness' (Daisley, 2022 p106). Where do you provide opportunities to learn the mastery of these elements in your class(es)?

Personal management – This links to the teaching of fortitude but is also about how you enable children and young people to learn how to manage themselves, their learning and their possessions. This is particularly important for those who have abuse and trauma experiences as they often present with neuro atypical behaviours akin to attention-deficit hyper activity (ADHD) traits such as chaotic thinking, behaviour management, work approach and possession management. Thinking about how you can enable these children and young people to manage, the strategies you can teach and the scaffolding they will need in order to progress with their learning.

Critical thinking – A key element of being able to keep oneself safe is being able to discriminate between those who are genuine and those who are intending to harm. In order to do this, children and young people need to be able to analyse what is presented to them and work out who they can trust. Children and young people need to be helped to think about what those adults who mean to harm them are doing while they are in the grooming phase. In all subject areas and phases it is important to teach critical thinking skills that promote thinking about this, so how are you planning to teach these skills?

In teaching these things you enable the children and young people in your care to understand how important they are, what they should expect from relationships, how to manage when life is difficult, where they can go when they need help and how to look after themselves as they grow into adulthood.

In addition to these specific informal areas for teaching about safeguarding, there are many and varied ways in which you can contribute to children and young people learning about keeping themselves safe. Most of these will be ad hoc opportunities perhaps based on you being the person that a particular child or young person trusts – their key or trusted adult. They may also present themselves in the informal settings and conversations you have with children and young people around the school or when you have demonstrated a curiosity about their lives. In order to effectively safeguard children and young people in these situations you need to be alert to safeguarding issues that might need passing on to the Designated Safeguarding Lead (DSL). You need to be aware of when your knowledge or expertise in an area is not sufficient to teach or guide and you need to be honest with the children or young people you are engaging with. If you don't know, do not pretend you do but do not leave it there. Pursue the information that they need to keep safe and either revisit this with them when you have found out what they need to know or pass it on to the colleagues who are carrying out the formal teaching.

Case Study 10.1

Background
Two girls were chatting in Annie's class, they were talking about the club that they attended outside school. This club was one that a number of pupils in the school attended and was well known to staff. They were talking about a particular leader at this club and how he made them feel creepy.

Instead of asking the girls to be quiet and get on with the work she had asked them to do, Annie joined the conversation. She asked the girls who they were

(Continued)

talking about and why they felt creepy. She reminded them of characters in the books they had read and asked if the relationship they had with the club leader made them feel like any of these. She pushed them to think critically about both what they had read and what they had experienced to ensure she understood what they were experiencing but also so they could be empowered to judge for themselves.

What Happened?

The girls recognised that the creepiness that they were feeling was about how the club leader spoke to them and that this was not how an adult should speak to a child. Annie supported the girls to speak to the school's DSL.

The DSL made a referral to the Local Authority Designated Officer (LADO) to ensure that the behaviour of the adult in the club was challenged.

Reflective Questions

- How did Annie use this disclosure as an opportunity to teach about safeguarding?
- What safeguarding issues can you identify?
- How might you apply this case study/learning with the children and young people that you work with?

Your Approach

Whether you are teaching the formal safeguarding curriculum or the informal one or both – you need to think about how you approach what is said and the implication this will have on your relationship with the child or young person.

You need to make sure that any personal bias or opinions are held in check to allow the child or young person to explore what they need to know in their safe relationship with you. This might mean that you need to think about what you are bringing to this space. It does not mean that you cannot have your own thoughts, opinions and beliefs. It does mean that if a child or young person expresses something that goes against these or something that is shocking to you, you need to respond empathically and put aside what you think. The following case study might show you how this might occur and how you might respond.

Case Study 10.2

Background

Anisa was a devout Muslim. She had overcome bias and discrimination in her own life and schooling in order to become a teacher and was determined that this would not prevent her from becoming the best that she could be. In her first teaching practice she was teaching in a school with children and young people from a wide range of backgrounds. Many of the young people behaved in a way which was at odds with Anisa's own beliefs about how people should behave.

While she was shadowing a teacher in tutor time she overheard one of the boys talking about a party that he had attended where there were older young people who were having sex while drunk.

What Happened?
Anisa recognised that this was something that she had no experience of and made sure that she thought carefully about how she passed this information on to the boy's tutor. She realised that the older young people may have been old enough to consent to sex so this should not concern her. She decided that her concern was that the boy had been at a party where there was lots of alcohol and that she was not in full possession of the facts and did not know if he had been safe at the party or not. She had this discussion with the tutor.

The tutor, who had a good relationship with the boy, had a conversation with him about what had been overheard. He told the tutor that he had felt unsafe and had felt that he had to drink in order to be part of the crowd. He said that he had not had sex but that some of the adults there had suggested they would 'fix him up' next time. He said he was scared of what might happen if he said no to going to the next party.

The tutor made an immediate referral to the DSL who, in discussion with the boy, made an immediate referral to children's social care.

Reflective Question
- What bias do you think that Anisa had to challenge?
- What safeguarding issues can you identify?
- How might you apply this case study/learning with the children and young people that you work with?

Teaching Through Being a Role Model

In Chapter Three, we explored how you need to remain boundaried with children to maintain a professional relationship. When we are talking about teaching children and young people to be safe in their worlds one of the key ways we can do this is by being a role model or by representing what they can be. We have already talked about children and young people who exhibit harmful sexual behaviours are more likely to have experienced chaotic and traumatic relationships including domestic abuse (see Chapter Two). We have thought about those children and young people who do not disclose abuse because this is their normal (Chapters Four and Six). For these children and young people how we conduct ourselves in all aspects of our role, including those that we do not think they see, is vital to support a different perspective of what is normal and how they should conduct themselves. Our own healthy lifestyles and life choices help children and young people to determine what they should be aiming for.

Supporting Children and Young People to Support Each Other

In teaching safeguarding to children and young people both formally and informally you are modelling how relationships should work. The best teachers in all ages and subjects encourage children and young people to support each other learning how to work together to find out what they need to know. Teaching about safeguarding is no exception. There is though one caveat. That is that if children and young people are supporting each other they need to know when to ask for help. Often disclosures come from the friend of the child or young person in difficulty as do concerns about the welfare of their peers – as we saw in the case study in 5.3. In teaching how to keep safe it is important that the systems to support those who are supporting each other are clear and reminders are frequent. Many schools now have child friendly safeguarding policies and the photos or contact details of the safeguarding team are displayed around the school – even in the toilets. If your school does not habitually do this, you might want to suggest it or at least make sure that in your classroom where children or young people can find help and support is publicised. This means not only the teams at school but other sources like Childline (NSPCC). At the end of this chapter you will find a list of helpful organisations with their contact websites. I would not have all of these on the wall of your classroom but it might be worth children or young people knowing that you are a source of this information and that you are happy to share it if they need support. If you are asked for it – always probe further and alert the DSL if only to flag that there may be a concern and the information you have passed on. As in Chapter Four, make sure that you are clear with the child or young person who you will be telling and why – never promise that you will keep secrets about safeguarding issues.

> ### Case Study 10.3 – Secondary Example
>
> #### Background
> Agnes was worried – her friend had told her that they were transgender some time ago and Agnes had helped them to speak to teachers about what they wanted to do. James as they were now known had socially transitioned at school with his parent's knowledge.
>
> All the way through Agnes had been someone who James could talk to or message on social media, often late into the evening. James' parents were struggling with their daughter becoming a son and James often vented his frustration with them in these conversations. Agnes was concerned that James

was not managing the emotions and family conflict around his transition very well and was beginning to feel anxious herself about what James was feeling and how he might manage this.

What Happened?
Agnes had a good relationship with her tutor, who was also James' tutor. She decided that she would confide in her tutor about her worries and ask her what she should do. The tutor was really supportive and gave Agnes space to talk about her worries about James and also her own increasing mental health challenges. They decided that the support that James needed was beyond what Agnes could offer. They spoke to the DSL together to ask him to support James with accessing ongoing emotional support so that Agnes could return to being James' friend. Removing the pressure of being his support Agnes felt less anxious and needed no further support herself. Her tutor made sure to check in with both of them from time to time to make sure that they were feeling supported.

Reflective Question
- How was Agnes supporting James?
- What do you think the tutor had done to ensure that Agnes knew when to speak to her?
- How did the teacher take a trauma informed approach to supporting Agnes?
- What safeguarding issues can you identify here?
- How might you apply this case study/learning with the children and young people that you work with?

Case Study 10.4 – Primary Example

Background
Cassie and Lukas were playing together in the Reception class outdoor kitchen. Lukas was still in the early stages of learning English but that did not matter for the mud pies and noise they were making. The teacher was heartened to hear the laughter that their games were causing, particularly as Lukas was generally quiet and had taken time to engage with the other children in the class.

What Happened?
Just as the teacher was returning inside Cassie came rushing up to her and told her that something had happened to Lukas and she needed to come. The teacher rushed over to Lukas only to find him still happily making mud pies. Cassie indicated the teacher to Lukas and demanded that he 'tell'. Lukas shyly turned to show the teacher some bruises on his arm which were only now visible where he had pushed up his sleeves to avoid getting muddy.

(Continued)

The teacher left the children in the care of the teaching assistant and went to get the DSL who spoke to Lukas and managed to get him to communicate that the marks had been caused by his mother grabbing his arm. The DSL then followed the school safeguarding policy to make a referral to Children's Social Care.

Reflective Question
- What support do you think Cassie might need after this, if any?
- Think about the culture in the Reception classroom – what do you think the teacher and teaching assistant have done to ensure that Cassie knows that bruises like Lukas' need her to speak to an adult?
- What safeguarding issues can you identify here?
- How might you apply this case study/learning with the children and young people that you work with?

Safeguarding Leadership

Some schools are now encouraging children and young people to be part of the leadership of safeguarding. This is to be encouraged as a real example of teaching children and young people how to both support and seek support. While you may not be able to influence the whole school approach to this you could provide opportunities in your classroom for children and young people to take responsibility for keeping each other safe by getting them to contribute to: the building of relationships (Chapter Three); classroom well-being strategies (Chapter Four); spotting behaviour changes in others (Chapter Five) and creating a safe environment (Chapter Eight).

Case Study 10.5

Background
In the school that Olivier was teaching in safeguarding champions had just been introduced. One of the children in his class had been given the role and was working hard to present an assembly on 'stranger danger' for the children in key stage one. Olivier had also been briefed about providing emotional support to the child if it was needed. Having presented the assembly, the child in Olivier's class and another child in the partner class were going out onto the key stage one playground in case any of the younger children wanted to talk to them.

What Happened?
When the child returned to Olivier's class he looked worried. Olivier made sure to ask what was wrong. The child told him that one of the key stage one children had told him that there was a stranger in the alleyway on the way into school and that they

were scared. The child also told Olivier that he was now scared to walk home as he walked down that alleyway on his own. Olivier reassured the child that he had done the right thing and said that he would make sure that he was safe on the way home.

Olivier reassured the child and spoke to the DSL who spoke to the local Police Community Support Officers (PSCOs). They agreed to make sure that they were on duty in the alley that day and that they would ensure that the 'stranger' was 'moved on' permanently to ensure the safety of the children on their way into school.

Reflective Questions
- What did Olivier do to support the safeguarding champion in his class?
- What safeguarding issues can you identify here?
- How might you apply this case study/learning with the children and young people that you work with?

Teaching Online Safety

In the next chapter we will explore online safety in more detail. As online issues are now so pervasive it is important for every teacher to reinforce the safety messages that are taught in RSE/RHSE/PHSE and assemblies. This means that whatever phase or subject you are teaching you know what messages to teach children both explicitly and implicitly through your lessons. Read the next chapter to find out about the issues facing children and young people and make sure you keep up to date with what you can do to help.

Organisations That You Can Signpost Children and Young People to for Support

https://www.nspcc.org.uk/keeping-children-safe/reporting-abuse/nspcc-helpline/
https://www.mind.org.uk/for-young-people/
https://www.childrenssociety.org.uk/information/young-people
https://www.youngminds.org.uk/
https://www.barnardos.org.uk/get-support/support-for-young-people
https://www.childline.org.uk/
https://www.papyrus-uk.org/
https://centrepoint.org.uk/do-you-need-help/i-need-help-now/im-under-18
https://coramvoice.org.uk/

Summary for This Chapter

In this chapter, we have learnt about the issues children need to know and how they are taught about it – we have looked briefly at the formal curriculum and also the informal curriculum that every teacher should take responsibility for. We have also explored how children and young people can be encouraged to take responsibility for their own safeguarding and that of their peers. How you can encourage pupil leadership is also touched on. Teaching online safety is briefly introduced and will be further explored in Chapter Eleven.

References

Burr, R. (2022) *Self-Worth in Children and Young People*. Plymouth: Critical Publishing.

Daisley, B. (2022) *Fortitude: The Myth of Resilience, and the Secrets of Inner Strength*. Texas: Cornerstone Press.

Department for Education (DfE) (2013) *Citizenship Programmes of Study: Key Stages 3 and 4 National Curriculum in England*. Available at: https://assets.publishing.service.gov.uk/media/5f324f7ad3bf7f1b1ea28dca/SECONDARY_national_curriculum_-_Citizenship.pdf [Accessed 17.3.24].

Department for Education (DfE) (2019) *Statutory Guidance Relationships and Sex Education (RSE) and Health Education*. Available at: https://www.gov.uk/government/publications/relationships-education-relationships-and-sex-education-rse-and-health-education [Accessed 17.3.24].

Department for Education (DfE) (2024) *Keeping Children Safe in Education*. London: DfE. Available at: https://www.gov.uk/government/publications/keeping-children-safe-in-education–2 [Accessed 26.5.24].

UK Government (1989) *Children Act 1989, c. 41*. London: HMSO. Available at: www.legislation.gov.uk/ukpga/1989/41/contents [Accessed 26.3.24].

UNICEF (n.d.) *A Summary of the UN Convention on the Rights of the Child*. Available at: https://www.unicef.org.uk/wp-content/uploads/2019/10/UNCRC_summary-1_1.pdf [Accessed on 9.3.24].

11
Online Safety

Chapter Aims

- To introduce online safety.
- To explore the responsibilities of teachers with respect to filtering and monitoring.
- To explore how young people are groomed online, what the risks are and what that might look like in the classroom.
- To think about issues teachers might encounter between children and young people.
- To reinforce messages about online safety for teacher's personal and professional integrity.

Introduction

This chapter looks at the very real problems that teachers encounter not only in the classroom but beyond it in terms of online safety. It explores the issues around keeping children and young people safe on school networks and the issues children and young people encounter with each other both in school and out of school that impact on relationships with peers. It also covers the role of the teacher in providing and reinforcing messages about how to keep safe online and how teachers can do this for themselves to protect their personal and professional identity.

Online Safety – An Introduction

Online safety is a rapidly growing and rapidly changing area of safeguarding with children and young people at increasing levels of risk. In fact, Baginsky et al. (2022) suggest that it is the fastest growing area of challenge in safeguarding for schools. Online safety in schools, according to their research ranges from

> extreme violence as well as a range of mental health concerns resulting from inappropriate or harmful online material involving self-harm, suicide and disorder sites. (Baginsky et al., 2022 p76)

There are also increasing concerns about the exposure of children and young people – especially males – to online pornographic material and misogyny with the Children's Commissioner (2023) suggesting that this is the source for increasing levels of harmful sexual behaviour by children and young people.

Keeping Children Safe in Education (Department for Education (DfE), 2024) suggests that all staff should receive online safety training as part of their induction and that this should be regularly updated. This should help you to keep up to date with this rapidly changing area. Some schools will include online safety within their child protection or safeguarding policy while others will have a separate policy. This should be given to you on induction as we saw in Chapter One, make sure you read it as it will help you to understand the school's expectations in terms of both your behaviour and that of children and young people online.

More generally you should know that the Online Safety Bill was finally passed in 2023 and this should enable the better protection of children and young people online. At the time of writing there is still some determination about how it will be implemented to ensure that tech companies do more to prevent online grooming, issues related to inappropriate information (such as those related to eating disorders, knife crime and suicide) and child abuse images online. Given the speed at which risks and issues online change and develop it is important that you make sure that you are as up to date as you can be in both your knowledge and understanding. There are a number of internet sites where you can find out more about current issues with regards to online safety. Please do use them to be well informed, some are listed here but there are many more! If you use ones other than this, make sure that you critically analyse them and the information that they present you with. This is particularly important if you are going to use the information with children or young people.

- The NSPCC https://www.nspcc.org.uk/keeping-children-safe/online-safety/
- Internet Watch Foundation https://www.iwf.org.uk/
- UK Safer Internet Centre https://saferinternet.org.uk/
- South West Grid for Learning https://swgfl.org.uk/
- Internet Matters https://www.internetmatters.org/
- INEQUE https://ineqe.com/online-safety/
- National Online Safety https://nationalcollege.com/parents

In addition to the now more traditional areas of online safety the increasing usage of Artificial Intelligence (AI) is a growing concern. The ability to be able to create and present information and both static and live images is hugely concerning, particularly when children and young people do not question whether what they are being presented with is true, and hence the need for all teachers to teach about critical thinking in all phases (see Chapter Ten). How children and young people use AI in child-on-child abuse is also a growing issue.

Filtering and Monitoring

In 2023, Filtering and Monitoring Standards were introduced, entitled *Meeting Digital and Technology Standards in Schools and Colleges* (DfE, 2023), these detail all the responsibilities that schools have for keeping children and young people safe online. You do not need to know all the finer details as the Designated Safeguarding Lead (DSL) will take responsibility for overseeing this with final accountability resting with the governor or trustees. There are, however, some key aspects that you need to know as a member of staff to make sure you report any breaches to the filtering and monitoring system that your school has adopted. You need to report to the DSL or sometimes to the IT lead if you:

- Witness or suspect unsuitable material has been accessed by children or young people (if you suspect an adult in school has accessed such material this falls under allegations management and should be referred to the Head Teacher in the first instance).
- Inadvertently access unsuitable material – see below.
- Are teaching topics which could create unusual activity on the filtering logs for example you are teaching sex education or PHSE/RSE topics.
- Identify that there is failure in the software or abuse of the system, for example there has been a breach of the protection systems or some errant software has allowed access to the system.
- Come across perceived unreasonable restrictions that affect teaching and learning or administrative tasks – some systems are hypersensitive and can restrict both you and children or young people from accessing learning material.
- Notice abbreviations or misspellings that allow access to restricted material – some sites deliberately mimic areas of learning that children or young people might be searching in order provide access.

If you inadvertently access something inappropriate on the school's system, it is important that you report this as soon as you possibly can. Most filtering and monitoring reports will highlight this in any case and may mean you find yourself being investigated under low-level concern or allegations management procedures. If you are able to pre-empt this by reporting yourself, it will greatly help your case than if it is discovered through a formal report. You also need to make sure that if you are using your own equipment on the school's network (e.g. phones or iPads) or if you are using school equipment at home on your own Wi-Fi that you have not left open any tabs that might be considered to be inappropriate. These continue to run in the background and can also trigger the filtering and monitoring system causing you to have to answer some difficult questions as to whether you have been accessing material that the school views unfavourably via the school network. You may think that this is unlikely but a number of teachers have been identified as viewing pornography at home because of open tabs; as have partners of teachers who have used equipment at home and left the last page they visited open, before the equipment is taken back into school.

> ### Case Study 11.1
>
> ### Background
> Grace had been asked to teach a PHSE about misogyny and relationships with girls and women in response to a few issues with the boys in her Year Six class. She knew it was an important topic to get right and so she decided to research carefully before talking to her mentor about the lesson.
>
> In searching for information about and the perpetrators of extreme misogyny Grace found some useful information about incels – these are usually males who think of themselves as being involuntarily celibate. As a result, they can show extreme hostility towards women – particularly those who think of themselves as active. In following a link about these individuals Grace found herself in a chat room where there were a number of conversations going on that Grace found distressing. She immediately closed the browser.
>
> ### What Happened?
> Grace was really worried about what she had seen and the fact that she could access this on the school network. She decided to discuss it with her mentor, who recommended that she report it immediately to the DSL and the network manager.
>
> Grace was relieved to have passed on the information, particularly as the DSL told her that he had already received a notification about the access of the site and would have had to follow it up more formally if Grace had not explained how the site was accessed by accident and how distressing she had found it. The network manager made sure that the site was added to the blocked sites for the school network.
>
> ### Reflective Questions
> - What did Grace do to safeguard herself and the children and young people in the school?
> - What safeguarding issues can you identify?
> - How might you apply this case study/learning with the children and young people that you work with?

Online Grooming

'Grooming is a word used to describe people befriending children in order to take advantage of them for sexual abuse and other forms of child abuse'. (Internet Matters, n.d. n.p.). When children or young people are online they are more likely to come across people who are not who or what they say they are than when they meet people in 'real life'. This is becoming even more prevalent with the advent of sophisticated AI programmes that enable people to present themselves as anyone they chose online, even over a screen. A number of organisations including the Internet Watch Foundation produce figures that show how many children and young people are coerced by groomers to share images of themselves nude or semi-nude. There are also a number of horrific stories of children or young people being persuaded to meet groomers. In some instances, the groomers have been so effective the child or young person willingly goes to meet someone who they think will treat them well. Sometimes the child or young person goes to meet someone and the groomer is not who they expect to see. In either scenario meeting a groomer is often fatal. There are examples of this that have been made into films to help children and young people see the dangers of online grooming and many schools use these as part of the learning that children need around keeping themselves safe.

Case Study 11.2

This case study is one that you can find on YouTube and illustrates just how dangerous grooming can be – you may find it upsetting. Please make sure you reach out to colleagues or friends for support if you do.

Background
Kayleigh was an average teenager with a happy family life. One evening she received a message online asking how she was. She responded and after some messaging that drew her in to thinking the person who had messaged was someone she could talk to she sent the person on the other end her telephone number. The messages continued, and she began to spend more time alone in her room 'talking' to the person on the other end of the text messages.

Eventually he persuaded her to meet him, Kayleigh thought her parents would not understand this relationship and lied to them about where she was going to stay the night. By this time Kayleigh was so enthralled she thought he was her 'one' and went along with the alcohol he plied her with and the sex that he wanted. He told her that he wanted her to meet his friends – she thought that meant he was serious about her.

What Happened?
When the perpetrators friends arrived and also wanted sex. Kayleigh tried to run away. The perpetrator followed her and killed her.

A film about Kayleigh has been made by Leicestershire Police which can be viewed on YouTube at the following link: https://www.youtube.com/watch?v=WsbYHI-rZOE.

Reflective Questions
- What might you have seen at school when Kayleigh was becoming more and more involved with this online 'relationship'?
- What safeguarding issues can you identify?
- How might you apply this case study/learning with the children and young people that you work with?

What to Look Out For

Online grooming is extremely hard to spot as by its nature it is, at least in the initial stages, conducted in private. The online worlds of children and young people are more and more extensive and keeping track of what they are doing is often difficult. For a child or young person that you know well it might be that you spot changes in behaviour that can indicate that they are developing an unhealthy online relationship with someone who is a groomer. These are likely to include being more secretive, becoming isolated from peers, a previously diligent pupil becoming less so. If the groomer has moved onto asking for explicit photographs you may see a child or young person changing their appearance. If the groomer has moved on to meeting in person or the child or young person has shared their address you might see gifts that have been given. As a teacher your role is to prevent children and young people from being groomed in the first place. This will be as part of the PHSE or RSE curriculum but also as part of your regular interaction with them through the modelling of positive relationships and the teaching of critical thinking as we discussed in Chapter Ten.

If you see initial signs that prevention has not been successful, then you should share this with the DSL and they will advise next steps. **Never** try and access the electronic devices of children or young people. You must also never investigate someone that you think might be trying to groom a child or young person – these people are criminals and some can be very dangerous individuals.

Online Safety Issues Between Children and Young People

Children and young people are not always nice to each other. As a teacher you will see this in the classroom and will develop strategies for managing this as well as application of the school's behaviour or relationship policy. When the issues children or young people have with each other result in online interactions they can spill over into school life and can prove difficult resolve. One of the problems is that whatever happens online can be shared quickly with a large number of other people, leading to whole classes, year groups or schools knowing what has is happening before teachers are aware that there is an issue. The online issues between children or young people fall into the category of child-on-child abuse, which you might hear referred to as peer-on-peer abuse. This is a really serious category on abuse as both parties are likely to suffer or have suffered from harm.

Sexting

One of the key areas of online 'child-on-child' abuse is referred to as sexting. Sexting involves sending texts, images or videos that are sexual in nature by phone or online and is illegal for those under 18. So if children or young people in your school send images of themselves or others it means that they have broken the law. Reinforcing this is something that all those who work with children and young people need to do. Despite the education that goes into prevention, it appears that the disconnect from executive function that teenagers in particular experience means that there are still a significant number of children and young people who get themselves into trouble.

> ## Case Study 11.3
>
> ### Background
> Ellie and Andreas were both 16 years old and in a relationship. They had made it clear to everyone at school that they were sexually active and the DSL alongside Claire, who was their form tutor, spoke to both about consent and about contraception. They had explained that they were in love, that they were not stupid and knew what to do to prevent Ellie becoming pregnant. The DSL had asked if their parents knew that they were sexually active. Andreas' parents knew but Ellie said that her Dad would not understand and exercised her rights to confidentiality as she was not at risk of harm. The DSL made sure that both young people knew that they could talk to her or Claire at any time if they needed to.
>
> ### What Happened?
> One morning in tutor period Andreas and Ellie were not sitting together and Ellie looked tearful. Before she went to lessons Claire asked what was wrong. Ellie explained that she and Andreas had split up and she was upset that he had said that he would not delete the photos she had sent to him.
>
> Claire knew that this was serious and immediately alerted the DSL who was able to remove Andreas from his lesson and ask about the photos. The DSL was able to ensure that Andreas had not already shared the photos and make sure that he had deleted them from his phone.
>
> Claire and the DSL then spoke to both Ellie and Andreas about the dangers of taking and sharing images and the fact that what they had done was illegal and also made their separation more difficult.
>
> ### Reflective Questions
> - What might you have been able to do to prevent this from happening?
> - What safeguarding issues can you identify?
> - How might you apply this case study/learning with the children and young people that you work with?

Teachers have a role in identifying where there might be issues in relationships between children and young people. The sooner these can be managed in school the better as then they are less likely to spill over into online issues. It is not always possible to do this so do not blame yourself if a child or young person in your class is subsequently a victim or perpetrator of this kind of online abuse.

Online Safety for Teacher's Personal and Professional Integrity

In Chapter Three, we introduced your professional integrity in terms of relationships and then in Chapter Four we provided guidance about how to make sure that your electronic communication was professional. Here we reiterate how important it is to make sure that you maintain the boundaries in all your online communications – not only for the children and young people you teach but for all children and young people with yourself as well.

First of all, make sure that all your social media is 'locked down' so that only the people you have accepted as friends and contacts can see what you have posted. Then ensure that you only accept connection requests from people you know. Children and young people are just as capable of posing as someone they are not as adults in order to access your private world. Some schools even suggest that you use a name that is unlikely to be discoverable by children, young people and their families. This helps protect you from unwanted connection requests but is not infallible – so you need to act carefully.

If you have a LinkedIn profile or other professional profile that is more open – make sure what you post there is professional and would not cause you any embarrassment at school. You also need to make sure, as we mentioned earlier in this chapter, that you display integrity in your own use of the internet. You will make your own choices about your behaviour outside of school. Make sure that these do not mean that what you are doing is illegal. Make sure that all your behaviour is legal and this applies online too. While this may seem obvious you saw in Case Study 4.7 how teachers still get themselves into trouble. You should also ensure that you are not getting drawn into interactions online that display immoral activity – these too are likely to jeopardise your career as a teacher when they come to light. You will not be able to keep them hidden indefinitely.

If you have posts on your social media accounts that might be considered difficult in school then you may want to 'tidy up' your profiles now. In 2022, *Keeping Children Safe in Education* suggested that as part of their safer recruitment process schools and colleges 'should consider carrying out an online search as part of their due diligence on the shortlisted candidates' (DfE, 2024 p59). While not all schools have adopted this guidance in full and number have and will ask if they can check your public posts for illegal content, content that suggests you have extreme views, content that is deriding of any individual or former employer and so on. Some schools do this themselves but many now use organisations who use effective systems to trawl all of your online footprint. You have to consent to this check. Refusing consent however may be perceived as a barrier to your employment as would any negative discoveries. There is more about this in Chapter Four.

Teachers hold an important role in society. Make sure that your online behaviour enables you fulfil this role.

Summary for This Chapter

In this chapter, we have thought about your responsibilities in respect of the filtering and monitoring standards. We have also looked at an example of how children and young people are groomed online, what the risks are and what that might look like in your classroom. We have explored the online issues you might encounter between children and young people, particularly in relation to sexting. We have also reinforced messages about online safety for your personal and professional integrity.

References

Baginsky, M., Driscoll, J., Purcell, C., Manthorpe, J. and Hickman, B. (2022) *Protecting and Safeguarding Children in Schools*, Bristol: Policy Press.

Children's Commissioner (2023) *New Evidence on Pornography's Influence on Harmful Sexual Behaviour Among Children*. Available at: https://www.childrenscommissioner.gov.uk/media-centre/new-evidence-on-pornographys-influence-on-harmful-sexual-behaviour-among-children/ [Accessed 28.3.24].

Department of Education (2023) *Meeting Digital and Technology Standards in Schools and Colleges*. Available at: https://www.gov.uk/guidance/meeting-digital-and-technology-standards-in-schools-and-colleges/filtering-and-monitoring-standards-for-schools-and-colleges [Accessed 16.12.23].

Department for Education (DfE) (2024) *Keeping Children Safe in Education*. London: DfE. Available at: https://www.gov.uk/government/publications/keeping-children-safe-in-education–2 [Accessed 26.5.24].

Internet Matters (n.d) Available at: https://www.internetmatters.org/issues/online-grooming/learn-about-it/ [Accessed 16.12.23].

Conclusion

This book has collected together a range of safeguarding issues that you will have to manage in your classroom in order to get on with the business of teaching. You will need to be brave to face some of the experiences children and young people have lived through but you will do it for them and their futures. In thinking about safeguarding first you might be the person who makes the difference for them. This message shows how much of a difference you can make:

> I wanted to message you to tell you that I am so grateful I had a figure like you in my life. I'm glad I had a role model and someone that understood me and didn't gaslight me about what I was going through. You were one of the few adults in my life that made me feel safe, loved and validated and I'll never forget that. (Innes-Turnill, 2024 p294)

Let's return to the responsibilities for safeguarding from Chapter One, these are contained in the *Teachers' Standards* (DfE, 2011). We asked you to consider which ones were relevant to safeguarding and said we would return to them at the end of the book. Have another look at them here now:

> ### Teachers' Standards: Part Two: Personal and Professional Conduct
>
> Teachers uphold public trust in the profession and maintain high standards of ethics and behaviour, within and outside school, by:
>
> - treating pupils with dignity, building relationships rooted in mutual respect, and at all times observing proper boundaries appropriate to a teacher's professional position;
> - having regard for the need to safeguard pupils' well-being, in accordance with statutory provisions;
> - showing tolerance of and respect for the rights of others;
> - not undermining fundamental British values, including democracy, the rule of law, individual liberty and mutual respect and tolerance of those with different faiths and beliefs;
> - ensuring that personal beliefs are not expressed in ways which exploit pupils' vulnerability or might lead them to break the law.
>
> Teachers must have proper and professional regard for the ethos, policies and practices of the school in which they teach, and maintain high standards in their own attendance and punctuality.
>
> *(Continued)*

> Teachers must have an understanding of, and always act within, the statutory frameworks which set out their professional duties and responsibilities.
> (DfE, 2011 p14)
>
> ### Reflective Questions
> - Which ones do you think are relevant to safeguarding now?
> - Is this different from what you thought when you read Chapter One?

Your role as part of the safeguarding team is vital (Chapter One). You need to be confident in your knowledge and understanding of the issues children and young people face (Chapter Two). Building relationships (Chapter Three) with children and young people with safeguarding or trauma needs and supporting them to achieve is a huge privilege and one that will leave you and them changed. Learning how to communicate with children, young people, parents, carers and colleagues is a key part of making sure that you keep everyone safe (Chapter Four) as is making sure that you look after and keep yourself safe (Chapter Five). Understanding behaviour, learning to find out what drives it will make you a better teacher and safeguarding practitioner (Chapter Six) and will enable you to think about which emotionally sensitive strategies you adopt in order to address the issues that children and young people face (Chapter Seven). Making sure that the environment you teach in is as safe as possible for both you and the children and young people you teach will support this (Chapter Eight). Knowing how to provide help and support at the earliest possible stage may mean that you are able to reduce the long-term impact of safeguarding issues, abuse or trauma (Chapter Nine). Teaching about safeguarding and in particular critical thinking could support children and young people to recognise what has happened to them or even prevent the harm from happening in the first place (Chapter Ten). This is particularly important in the online world, where you too need to be careful (Chapter Eleven).

Most of all, if you think a child or young person is at risk of harm or has been harmed you must report it and get that child or young person help. This is everyone who works with children or young people's fundamental responsibility. Make sure you know how to do this before you step into a classroom and keep that at the front of your mind while you teach.

References

Department for Education (DfE) (2011) *Teachers' Standards*. London: DfE. Available at: https://assets.publishing.service.gov.uk/media/5a750668ed915d3c7d529cad/Teachers_standard_information.pdf [Accessed 12.11.23].

Innes-Turnill, D. (2024) 'Safeguarding'. In Forster, C. and Eperjesi, R. (eds.) *Introduction to Primary School Teaching*. London: SAGE.

Index

Abuse, 10, 33, 49, 50, 87
  alcohol, 129
  child-on-child, 22, 25–27
  contextual, 54
  domestic, 23, 129–130
  drug, 129
  emotional, 19
  honour-based, 131–132
  neglect, 20–22
  online, 22–23
  peer-on-peer, 22, 25–27
  physical, 18–19
  sexual, 19–20
  teenage relationship, 23
Academic curriculum, 34
Academic learning, 115
Accountability, 5, 6, 155
Acknowledging shame, 100
Adverse Childhood Experiences (ACEs), 41, 80, 93, 100, 102–103
Affection, 35–36
Ainsworth, M., 103
Alcohol abuse, 129
Allegations, 8, 18, 55
  management and low-level concerns, 28–30
  safeguarding, 61
Ambivalent attachment, 106–107
Amygdala, 94
ANS. *See* Autonomic nervous system (ANS)
Anxious attachment, 106–107
Appearance, dramatic change in, 53
Article 2 (non-discrimination), 143
Article 3 (best interests of the child), 143
Article 6 (life, survival and development), 143
Article 12 (respect for views of the child), 143
Article 13 (freedom of expression), 143
Article 14 (freedom of thought, belief and religion), 143
Article 19 (protection from violence, abuse and neglect), 144
Article 28 (right to education), 144
Article 29 (goals of education), 144
Article 39 (recovery from trauma and reintegration), 144
Artificial intelligence (AI), 154
Assault by penetration, 20
Attachment, 103
  ambivalent, 106–107
  anxious, 106–107
  avoidant, 104–106
  awareness, 104–108
  concept of, 103–104
  disorder, 88–89
  disorganised, 107–108
  disorientated, 107–108
  needs, 41
Attendance lead, 10–11
Autonomic nervous system (ANS), 111, 112
Avoidant attachment, 104–106
Avoiding shame, 101

Baginsky, M., 153
Behaviour Management Policy, 34
Behaviours, 2, 17
  attachment disorder, 88–89
  automatic, 50
  bias, 90–91
  bullying, 41
  children and young people, 81–88
  as communication, 79–91
  dramatic change in, 53
  ensuring, 76
  extremist, 23–25
  harmful sexual, 25
  low-level concern, 29
  physical, 25
  radicalisation, 23–25
  types of, 80–81
Belonging, 76
Bombèr, L. M., 104
Bowlby, J., 103
Brailsford, D., 66
Brain
  memory centre, 96
  parts of, 94, 95 (figure)
  plasticity, 96
Breathing exercises, 67
Bruises, 53
Brummer, J., 33
Bullying, 19, 119
  online, 22
  prejudice-based, 22
Burr, R., 39

Calming rituals, 67, 73
Chair of Governors, 29

Chief Executive Officer (CEO), 8
Child criminal exploitation, 22
Child in Care (CIC), 28
Child in need plan (CIN plan), 28, 86
Child Looked After (CLA), 28
Child-on-child abuse, 18, 22, 25–27, 54, 58, 115, 154, 158. *See also* Sexting
Child Poverty Action Group (CPAG), 129
Child protection, 61, 134
  legislation, 15
  policy, 3
  safeguarding and, 16–17
  threshold, 4, 5
Child Protection Online Management System (CPOMS), 56
Child Protection Plan (CP plan), 27
Children Act (1989), 17, 18, 123
  Section 17, 28
  Section 47, 27–28
Children Act (2004), 18
Children and young people, 3, 5, 7, 10, 11, 49
  accept, 85
  antisocial or criminal behaviour, 127–128
  appearance, dramatic change in, 53
  behaviours, 53, 81–88
  bruises or injury, 53
  class teacher relationships, 40–43
  communication, 53–54
  difficult conversations, 58, 59
  domestic abuse, 23
  drugs themselves, 130
  emotional abuse, 19
  exploited, 128
  family circumstance, 128–130
  family member in prison, 128
  grooming, 23
  honour-based abuse, 131–132
  making mistakes, 115–116
  mental health needs, 125–126
  misusing alcohol, 130
  neglect, 20
  notice, 83, 84
  online safety, 158–159
  organisations, 151
  pause, 83, 85
  physical abuse, 19
  radicalised, 128
  regulation, 83–88
  reliability, 38
  repair, 85–86
  respect, 37–38
  rights education, 143–144
  safeguarding, 139–152
  self-worth, 39–40
  sexual abuse, 19, 20
  support each other, 148–150
  thinking, 83, 85
  trust, 36–37
  understand, 85
  well-being, 70, 72–74, 76
  young carers, 126–127
Children's Commissioner, 154
Children's Social Care National Framework, 17
Child sexual exploitation, 22
Child social care (CSC), 27
Citizenship curriculum, 139, 140
Class teacher, 2–5
  carers, 41–42
  children, 40–41
  local community, 43–44
  other professionals, 43
  other staff, 41
  parents, 41–42
  relationships, 40–44
  responsibility examples, 4
  standards, 2–3
Clinical supervision, 70
Code of conduct, 2, 3
Communication, 2, 33, 49–63
  behaviours as, 79–91
  children and young people, 49, 52–53
  digital and social media, 61–63
  disclosure. *See* Disclosure
  electronic, 59
  elements of, 58
  lack of, 53–54
Conradi, L., 98, 112
Contextual abuse, 54
Contextual safeguarding, 27, 58
Co-regulation, 87
Cozolino, L., 34, 103, 112, 120
Critical thinking, 145–146
Curriculum, 38
  academic, 34
  citizenship, 139
  formal, 139–143
  informal, 144–146
  safeguarding teaching opportunities, 141–142 (table)
Cyberbullying, 19

Daisley, B., 144
Deputy Designated Safeguarding leads (DDSLs), 6, 7, 19
Designated Safeguarding Lead (DSL), 5, 19, 51, 86, 123, 145, 155
  emotional abuse, 19
  neglect, 20
  physical abuse, 19
  questions to ask, 7
  record keeping, 5
  safeguarding team and, 5–7
  sexual abuse, 20
  telling, 55–56

Designated Teacher, 10
Difficult conversations, 58–60
Difficult relationships, 44–45
Digital media, 61–63
Disabilities, 10
Disclosure, 50–52, 51 (figure), 54–55
   Designated Safeguarding Lead, 55–56
   distressing, 67
   recording, 56–58
Disorganised attachment, 107–108
Disorientated attachment, 107–108
Distress, 80–81
Document checklist, 13
Dolezal, L., 100
Domestic abuse, 23, 129–130
Domestic Abuse Act (2021), 129
Dorsal vagal, 112
Dramatic change
   in appearance, 53
   in behaviour, 53
DSL. *See* Designated Safeguarding Lead (DSL)
Dysregulation, 87

Early Career Framework (ECF), 72
Early Career Teacher (ECT), 6
Early help, 4, 123–136
   assessment tools, 133–136
   partnerships, 132–133
   processes, 123–132
Edmondson, A., 114
Educational Psychologists, 11
Education Health Care Plan (EHCP), 10, 124
Electronic communications, 59, 61
Emotional abuse, 19, 36
Emotionally sensitive strategies
   Adverse Childhood Experiences (ACEs), 102–103
   attachment, 103–108
   Maslow's Hierarchy of Needs, 108
   shame sensitive practice, 100–102
   trauma, 93–97
   trauma-informed classroom, 98–100
   trauma-informed practice, 97
Emotional resilience, 67
Emotional safety, 113–114
Emotion Coaching, 87
Empowerment, 98
Eperjesi, R., 73
Equality Act, 99, 119
Equality, Diversity and Inclusion, 119
Exclusion, 80
Extremism, 23
Extremist behaviour, 23–25
Fawn, 80

Female genital mutilation (FGM), 23, 131–132
Fight, 80

Filtering, monitoring and, 155–156
Firmin, C., 27
Flight, 80
Flop, 81
Forced marriage, 23, 131–132
Formal curriculum, 139–143
Forster, C., 73
Fortitude, 39, 144
Freeze, 80

Geddes, H., 88, 104
Gender-based violence, 22
General practitioner (GP), 68
Gibson, M., 100
Golding, K. S., 82
Governors, 9
Greene, R. W., 80, 89
Grooming, 23, 156–157

Harassment, 18
Harmful sexual behaviours, 25
Harming, 17, 18
Head Teacher (or Principal), 7–9, 29
Hippocampus, 96–97
Hoath, L., 73
Homelessness, 23
Honour-based abuse, 131–132
Honour-based violence, 23
Humiliation, 101
Hypothalamus, 94

Illegal drugs, 129
Impairment, 17
Informal curriculum, 144–146
   critical thinking, 145–146
   fortitude, 144
   personal management, 144–145
   resilience, 144
   self-esteem, 144
   self-regulation, 144
   self-worth, 144
Initial Child Protection Conference (ICPC), 27
Initial Teacher Training (ITT), 72
Injury, signs of, 53
Innes-Turnill, D., 129, 163
Internal working model (IWM), 103
Internet Watch Foundation, 157
The Invisible Classroom, 112

Joseph Rowntree Foundation, 129

Keeping Children Safe in Education (KCSIE), 1, 3–5, 11, 17–18, 22–23, 50, 58, 72, 99, 124, 154
Kindness, 36
Knowing, 50

Learning needs, 10
Learning pedagogy, 73
Legislation, 15, 18
Lewis, C., 58
The Light We Carry, 36
Limbic system, 94, 95 (figure)
LinkedIn, 160
Local Authority Designated Officer (LADO), 8, 29
Looked After Child (LAC), 10, 28

Maltreatment, 17
Maslow, A. H., 108, 109
Maslow before Bloom, 33
Maslow's Hierarchy of Needs, 33, 34 (figure), 108, 108 (figure)
Maté, G., 94
Maternal substance abuse, 20
MATs. *See* Multi Academy Trusts (MATs)
Mental health lead, 10–11
Mental health needs, 125–126
Microaggressions, 99, 119
Mindfulness, 67, 113
Multi Academy Trusts (MATs), 8
Multi-agency partners, 11, 124
Multi Agency Referral Form (MARF), 27
Multi Agency Safeguarding Hub (MASH), 26, 27, 58
My Concern, 56
My Plan, 10, 124

Negative self-conscious emotion, 100
Neglect, 10, 20–22, 36
Neurons, 96
Non-contact activities, 20
Non-penetrative acts, 20
Nutritious food, 66

Olson, K., 34, 103, 112, 120
Online abuse, 22–23
Online bullying, 22
Online safety, 153–161
 children and young people, 158–159
 filtering and monitoring, 155–156
 grooming, 156–157
 teacher's personal and professional integrity, 160
 teaching, 151
Online Safety Bill, 154
Organisational accountability, 6
Out of hours team, 58
Over-the-counter drugs, 129

Page, J., 35
Parasympathetic system, 111
Parental offending, 128
Pastoral teams, 6

Pearlman, B., 33
Peer-on-peer abuse, 22, 25–27
Pence, D. M., 98
Personal conduct, 2–3
Personal Education Plan (PEP), 28
Personal, Health and Sex Education (PHSE), 139
Personal management, 144–145
Physical abuse, 18–19
Physical behaviours, 25
Physical contact, 20
Physical safety, 116–118
Podesta, E., 73
Positive emotions, 72
Positive feelings, 76
Positive relationships, 33–36
 classroom, 35–36, 35 (figure)
 definitions of, 34
Post-traumatic shame, 100
Poverty, 128–129
Pregnancy, 20
Prejudice-based bullying, 22
Prevent Officer, 24
Professional conduct, 2–3
Professional love, 35–36
Professional network, 72
Professional relationships, 41, 45–46
Psychological safety, 114–115
Pupil Premium Coordinator, 13
Pupil premium funding, 13
Pupil voice, 119

Radicalisation, 23–25
Reflective supervision, 70
Relationship building, 33–47
 class teacher, 40–43
 difficult, 44–45
 local community, 43–44
 positive, 33–36
 professional, 45–46
Relationships and Sex Education (RSE), 139
Relationships, Health and Sex Education (RHSE), 139
Reliability, 38
Resilience, 39, 76, 113, 144
Respect, 37–38
Restorative justice, 85, 89
Review Child Protection Conference (RCPC), 28
Roffey, S., 76, 115
Role model, 147–148
Rosa, H., 38
Rowe, J., 70

Safeguarding
 child protection and, 16–17
 children and young people, 139–152
 communication, 49–63
 contextual, 27

foundations, 15–16
issues, 22
knowledge, 15–30
leadership, 150–151
other areas of, 22–23
policy, 3, 16
relationship building, 33–47
role in, 12–13
system in schools, 1, 2 (figure)
teaching assistants, 11
team, 1–13
training, 3
understanding, 15–30
vs. well-being, 74–75
Safety, 98
emotional, 113–114
Equality, Diversity and Inclusion, 119
going outside, 118
learning environment, 115–120
making mistakes, 115–116
movement, 118
neurobiology of, 111–112
parents and carers, 120
physical, 116–118
psychological, 114–115
pupil voice, 119
School well-being strategies and policies, 69
Self-esteem, 85, 144
Self-management, 85
Self-regulation, 144
Self-worth, 39–40, 85, 144
Self-Worth in Children and Young People, 39
Seligman, M., 72
Senior Leadership Team (SLT), 5
Sexting, 158–159
Sexual abuse, 19–20, 39
Sexual comments, 25
Sexual 'jokes,' 25
Sexual violence, 18, 22
Shame sensitive practice, 100
acknowledging, 100
addressing, 101–102
avoiding, 101
Siegel, D., 82
Significant harm, 17
SLT. *See* Senior Leadership Team (SLT)
Social media, 49, 61–63, 160
Special Educational Need Coordinators (SENCOs), 10, 75
Special Educational Needs (SEN), 126
Strategy meeting, 27
Sturt, P., 70
Substance abuse, 129
Substance misuse, 23
Supervision, 70–71
Suspension, 80
Sympathetic nervous system, 111

Taunting, 25
Teacher well-being, 65, 76
Teaching assistants, 11
Teenage relationship abuse, 23
Terrorism, 23
Thalamus, 94
Trafficking, 22
Trauma, 33, 49, 50, 67, 80, 87
amygdala, 94
definitions, 93–94
hippocampus, 96–97
Trauma-informed classroom
choice, 98
collaboration, 98
cultural consideration, 99–100
empowerment, 98
Trauma-informed practice, 97, 112–115
emotional safety, 113–114
psychological safety, 114–115
Trustworthiness, 37, 98

United Nations Convention on the Rights of the Child (UNCRC), 143
Upskirting, 23
Using Supervision in Schools, 70

Van der Kolk, B.A., 93
Ventral vagal, 112
Violence
gender-based, 22
honour-based, 23
sexual, 22

Well-being, 3, 49, 65–77
belonging, 76
children and young people, 72–74, 76
definition of, 72
ensuring behaviour, 76
feeling and behaving, 66–67
mindfulness and calming rituals, 67
positive feelings and resilience, 76
professional network, 72
safe environment, 76
vs. safeguarding, 74–75
school well-being strategies and policies, 69
staff and pupil, 65
strategies, 67–68
supervision, 70–71
teacher, 65, 76
values, 76
WhatsApp, 61
Wilson, C., 98, 112
Working Together to Safeguard Children, 1, 9, 11, 15, 27, 72

Printed in Great Britain
by Amazon